7.50

RISING UP TO PREACH THE GOSPEL

WITNESS LEE

Living Stream Ministry

Anaheim, CA • www.lsm.org

First Edition, November 2003.

ISBN 0-7363-2412-7

Published by

Living Stream Ministry
2431 W. La Palma Ave., Anaheim, CA 92801 U.S.A.
P. O. Box 2121, Anaheim, CA 92814 U.S.A.

Printed in the United States of America

03   04   05   06   07   08   09   /   9   8   7   6   5   4   3   2   1

CONTENTS

PREFACE

This book is composed of messages given by Brother Witness Lee in the Chinese-speaking meeting in Anaheim, California. Chapters one through four were spoken on the Lord's Days in September and October of 1984, and chapters five through seven were spoken on July 31 through August 2 of 1986. These messages were not reviewed by the speaker.

CHAPTER ONE

THE COMMISSION OF THE GOSPEL

(1)

Scripture Reading: Matt. 28:18-19; Mark 16:15; Rom. 1:14-15;
1 Cor. 9:16-23; 2 Tim. 4:2a; Matt. 25:24-30; Acts 8:1, 4

Hymns, #921 was written by Fanny Crosby, an American
sister who was blind. The first stanza of this hymn with its
chorus reads,

> Rescue the perishing,
>   Care for the dying,
> Snatch them in pity from sin and the grave;
>   Weep o'er the erring one,
>   Lift up the fallen,
> Tell them of Jesus the mighty to save.
>
>   Rescue the perishing,
>   Care for the dying;
>   Jesus is merciful,
>   Jesus will save.

For the Chinese hymnal we used the same tune and rewrote
the above stanza and chorus, using updated words and expressions to be sung in the meetings concerning the preaching of
the gospel. A literal translation of the Chinese adaptation
reads as follows:

> Rise up for the gospel!
>   Rescue the lost souls!
> Look! Thousands are perishing day by day!
>   Don't be without mercy!
>   Don't love your money!
> Let go and preach the gospel right away!

> Rise up for the gospel!
> Rescue the lost souls!
> How can your heart be like steel
> While they are dying?

The secret to singing a hymn for gospel preaching is the release of our spirit. For our spirit to be released, first of all we must be freed and uninhibited, though not unbridled. When we sing freely, our spirit is released and our heart is opened; then spontaneously we will preach the gospel to others. On the contrary, if our spirit is depressed and our heart is closed, we cannot preach the gospel.

THE SECRET TO PREACHING THE GOSPEL

Being "Thick-skinned"

In order to be gospel preachers, we have to learn a few points. First, we must be "thick-skinned." If we seriously look into this, we will see that those who have been able to bear fruit for the gospel have all been thick-skinned. People who are thin-skinned cannot preach the gospel, much less be fruitful. To have the impact of the gospel, we must have a "skin that is thicker than our soles." Not only so, while preaching the gospel, we must have a face like brass. If we do not have a face like brass, we cannot preach the gospel. I was not a gospel preacher by nature, but due to the Lord's mercy, I was forced out of my old nature to become a "crazy" preacher of the gospel for the Lord. Forty years ago, from 1940 until 1943, I was a real "gospel fanatic" passionately preaching the gospel for the Lord.

Speaking with a Wide-open Mouth

The second point we have to learn for preaching the gospel is to open our mouth widely to speak everywhere. It does not matter even if you speak wildly; as long as it is the gospel, there will still be the effect. If you intend to convince people by reasoning and therefore speak properly with eloquence and persuasion, you will tend to kill them with your speaking. In the past fifty years in China, the most effective gospel preacher was Dr. John Sung. I heard his preaching. While preaching the gospel, sometimes he jumped from the platform to the ground and then used someone as a steppingstone to jump back to the platform. His messages did not follow any logical order. Sometimes he screamed at people and scolded them, and occasionally he even made strange noises in his speaking. Nevertheless, his gospel preaching was very effective.

Releasing the Spirit

The third point that we have to learn in the preaching of the gospel is the release of the spirit. To preach the gospel, you must have a spirit that is so released and strong that if you faced the devil, you would convince even him to receive the gospel. This is the spirit of the gospel.

These are the three points related to the gospel—to be thick-skinned, to have an open mouth, and to have a released spirit. You should not be bashful. Some brothers are so "unmanly" in their preaching of the gospel that they appear to be more female than the females. They are timid and apprehensive of everything. In particular, they are afraid of offending others. Their preaching of the gospel is doomed to failure.

TESTIMONIES OF GOSPEL PREACHING

In January of 1933, Dr. Sung went to Chefoo to preach the gospel, and I went to listen to him. I could not help but shake my head when I listened to his preaching. He used the woman who had a flow of blood as an example (Mark 5:25-34). He drew a heart on the blackboard and said, "This is a human heart, and it is your heart, a black heart. Oh, I came and spoke about the precious blood washing man's heart, washing man's heart. You were moved and your heart became burning for the Lord. But a few days after I left, the burning ceased, and the flow of blood began—the precious blood flowing out, flowing out...." He interpreted the woman's flow of blood as the precious blood of Jesus. That was really a nonsensical speaking. Nevertheless, his speaking was very captivating. For one and a half hours he kept hammering on this subject— the precious blood washing our heart, and the precious blood flowing out of our heart. The hall was crowded with over a thousand people. I shook my head at his preaching because what he said was altogether inaccurate. The Bible tells us not that the blood of the Lord Jesus cleanses our heart but that it washes away our sins. Even though Dr. Sung's teaching was inaccurate, the audience was moved. Many went to the front weeping, and they confessed and repented, saying, "O Lord, my blood flowed out. O Lord!" By this we see that the effectiveness of the gospel lies not in reasoning but in the release of the spirit.

My intention is not to encourage you to speak inaccurate doctrines but to show you that you need to exercise your spirit. One time Dr. Sung went to preach the gospel at Hankow, and my second oldest sister went to listen to him. When she came back, she told us that after Dr. Sung had spoken for a while, he suddenly picked up a wooden stick and pointed at a young lady in the audience, saying, "You are someone's mistress!" The woman was infuriated and said within, "How can you Christians behave in this way? You invite people to come to hear the gospel, yet you rebuke them." In fact, she was a concubine, a mistress. She thought that someone had told Dr. Sung about her case, so she was angry and bitter. After she went home, however, the Spirit operated in her, saying, "Why do you blame the preacher? Consider, are you not a concubine? Are you not a sinner? Why do you hate the preacher?" Having been enlightened, she repented. The next day she went again to hear the gospel and was saved.

Therefore, I would like to tell you that when you preach the gospel, if you care only about speaking rightly and pleasingly, do not expect to lead people to salvation. This does not mean that I am encouraging you to not speak rightly and to rebuke people. What I mean is that you should take care of the spirit of gospel preaching and allow your spirit to be released. In preaching the gospel you cannot be like an old pedant with a stern expression and a snobbish attitude. Instead, to lead people to salvation you have to be thick-skinned and have an open mouth and a released spirit.

THE SPIRIT OF THE GOSPEL
BEING A SPIRIT OF BEING BESIDE ONESELF

The Chinese are naturally conservative and well-behaved, so when they meet together, everyone is reserved and proper. This is not to say that it is wrong to behave properly. However, often when you are well-behaved, you become stiff and rigid and therefore restrict, hold back, the spirit. This is wrong. Paul said that we Christians have to be beside ourselves before God and sober-minded before men (2 Cor. 5:13). To be sober-minded is to be self-controlled in love for others' good. We should be sober-minded before men, but have we ever been beside ourselves before God? When we are by ourselves and no one is around, are we beside ourselves before God? If we are, then when we come to the meeting, we do not need to shout loudly—the moment we pray, others will be able to sense that we are beside ourselves before God. Paul was sober-minded before men, but when he was alone before God, he was beside himself. He is our pattern.

By the Lord's mercy, I am a person who is often beside myself, a person who is often "crazy." Sometimes after praying only three or five sentences, I became crazy, overflowing with joy. I felt that God's grace is so great and His mercy so abundant that I could not help being crazy. If no one is with me, it does not matter if I do such things as rolling, jumping, prostrating, and turning somersaults. But once I come into your presence, I become sober-minded. I am bound by your eyes and restricted by human regulations. It is right to take care of others' feelings, but as Christians we should daily pray and be beside ourselves before God.

If you are a person who is beside yourself before God, you will not be reserved in the meetings. On the contrary, you will manifest some signs of "craziness." We can illustrate this with Peter, whose true identity was revealed by his Galilean accent (Matt. 26:73). If you are often beside yourself when you pray to God in private, then once you come to the meeting and open your mouth, your "crazy" speaking will reveal your true condition. This does not mean that you pray and sing with a loud voice. Instead, it means that you are full of praises, thanksgivings, psalms, hymns, and spiritual songs, and you are full of the power of the Holy Spirit. In this way, others will know that you are a person who has been crazy before God. This is because what truly is within you will be manifested. You cannot pretend to be crazy if you are not crazy.

The spirit of the gospel is a spirit of being beside ourselves. In order to have the spirit of the gospel, we need to be "crazy" in our spirit. Do not pay too much attention to rules, and do not care too much for others' feelings. Sometimes when we are sitting in the meetings, we look around at the brothers and the sisters and we feel embarrassed to do anything. Whenever we have this kind of consideration, our spirit is restricted and has no way out. I hope that whenever we meet, we would break all rules, rituals, and formalities, thereby letting our spirit be released.

WORLD HISTORY BEING COMPLETELY UNDER THE LORD'S GOSPEL

If we study world history with spiritual insight, we will see that since the ascension of the Lord Jesus, the entire world history has been completely under the direction of the Lord's gospel. It is the gospel that directs the world; it is not the world that directs the gospel. By the Lord's mercy, I have studied this matter a great deal. Actually, even before the birth of the Lord Jesus, the world situation was working in different ways to coordinate with the gospel. On the political side, approximately thirty years prior to the birth of the Lord Jesus the Roman Empire rose up and conquered the regions of North Africa and Egypt, thus unifying the entire region around the Mediterranean Sea, including Canaan, the good land. Therefore, when the Lord Jesus was about to be born, the political situation in that area was stable under the rule of the Roman tetrarchs and governors.

The Birth of the Lord Jesus

The conception of the Lord Jesus is a mysterious matter. He was conceived of the Holy Spirit in the womb of Mary. At that time Mary was already engaged to Joseph, but the marriage was yet to be consummated. Amazingly, they were both descendants of David. Joseph was a descendant of David's son Solomon, while Mary was a descendant of Nathan, another son of David. The two lines of David's descendants brought forth Joseph and Mary and were joined in their marriage. When these two were married, however, both were poor, so they lived in Nazareth, a despised city in Galilee, which was a despised region. For the presenting of the Lord Jesus in accordance to the law of Moses, they could afford to offer only a pair of turtledoves or two young doves, which represent the smallest offering (Luke 2:24; Lev. 12:8). This proves that they were a family in poverty.

According to the prophecy in the Old Testament, the Lord Jesus had to be born in Bethlehem (Micah 5:2), but at that time Joseph and Mary were residing in the city of Nazareth. Today we have airplanes, cars, and other modern means of transportation, but two thousand years ago it was not as convenient for people to travel. From Nazareth to Bethlehem was about seventy-five miles, which required a road trip of many days. Considering their financial condition, they would not have traveled this far to Bethlehem only to give birth to the Lord Jesus. If the Lord Jesus were to be born in Nazareth, however, the Old Testament prophecy could not have been fulfilled. Therefore, for the fulfillment of the prophecy, God prepared something for them under His sovereign authority. When Mary was great with child and about to give birth, Caesar Augustus, the emperor of the Roman Empire, sent out a decree for a census to be taken of all the inhabited earth. Therefore, all went to be registered, each to his own city. Joseph and Mary were of the house and family of David and were therefore people belonging to Bethlehem. As such, they had to travel many miles back to Bethlehem. Because many had come back, the town's inns were all occupied and there was no place for them. It was at such a time that the Lord Jesus was born (Luke 2:1-7).

Mary had been pregnant for nine months and was living in Nazareth with Joseph. Just when it was time for her to give birth, the emperor gave the decree to take a census, paving the way for the Lord Jesus to be born in Bethlehem. This proves that the Roman Empire's ruling the whole world was for the birth of the Lord Jesus, that He might truly be born in Bethlehem, the hometown of His ancestor David, in order to fulfill the prophecy in Micah chapter five.

The Crucifixion of the Lord Jesus

When an Israelite slaughtered a lamb for the Passover, the priest would first put two pieces of wood together, one horizontal and the other vertical, to make a cross. Then he would "crucify" the lamb with its front legs fastened to the horizontal piece of wood and its hind legs to the vertical piece. Finally, he would cut the lamb open from the chest to the abdomen. Thus, according to the type in the Old Testament, the Lord Jesus, who died as the Lamb of God for our redemption, also had to be crucified.

Until the time of the Roman Empire, in human history there had not been a people or nation that used the cross as a way to put people to death. Although in the Old Testament the children of Israel might hang an executed criminal on a tree (Deut. 21:22-23), that could not be considered crucifixion. After the unification of the Roman Empire, a law was enacted which imposed a death penalty by crucifixion on anyone convicted of a heinous crime. At the time the Lord Jesus was arrested and convicted by the Jews, according to the law in the Old Testament He could only be stoned to death. However, since the Jews had already lost their nation, they did not have the authority of execution. Instead, they had to turn the authority over to the Roman Empire. It was in this way that the biblical prophecy concerning the crucifixion of the Lord Jesus was fulfilled.

From the birth and death of the Lord Jesus we can clearly see how the Roman Empire was used by God to accomplish what He had spoken in the Old Testament concerning the Lord Jesus. The Lord's birth was a fulfillment of the prophecy in the Old Testament, and His death was a fulfillment of the type in the Old Testament. However, the circumstances of His birth and His death were arranged by God through the Roman Empire. Afterward, the Lord Jesus resurrected and ascended for the spread of His gospel to propagate Himself. The subject of the book of Acts is that after His resurrection, the Lord Jesus ascended to heaven, was enthroned, poured down Himself as the all-inclusive Spirit, and sent His disciples to preach the gospel everywhere for the producing of the churches and for the spreading and propagating of the kingdom of God.

GOD'S ARRANGEMENT OF THE ENVIRONMENT FOR THE PREACHING OF THE GOSPEL

We are all clear today that the preaching of the gospel has to be matched by a proper environment. For the spread of the gospel we need a peaceful situation, a free flow of traffic, and a common language.

A Peaceful Situation

The nation of Israel was unique. Moreover, the land of Canaan, which they occupied according to God's arrangement, was also unique. In terms of geography it was isolated, but in terms of transportation it was linked to all directions. Because of this, God raised up the Roman Empire to conquer all the civilized regions in Europe and to take over all the lands around the Mediterranean. Due to its strong political and military power, Rome was able to maintain a situation which was peaceful, stable, and safe.

A Free Flow of Traffic

The people and nations within the territories of the Roman Empire, though very complicated, were all under one rule. Therefore, no matter where the citizens went, they could travel freely throughout the empire without having to apply for passes. Not only so, history tells us that the Roman Empire, after its unification, actively engaged itself in building highways from Rome to countries all around. It also put an end to the pirating activities on the Mediterranean Sea. As a result, traffic on the land and on the sea flowed freely and conveniently.

A Common Language

Before the establishment of the Roman Empire, about three hundred years before Christ, Greek became the language commonly spoken in the Jewish and Egyptian regions due to the conquest by Alexander the Great. After the unification of the Roman Empire, the government also picked up the usage of Greek and promoted the Greek culture as well. Thus, Greek culture became prevailing everywhere, and all language barriers were torn down. This shows us that all the environments are arranged by God for the spread of the gospel.

THE WORLD SITUATION GOING ALONG WITH THE GOSPEL

If we study the book of Acts and observe world history, we can realize that the world situation always goes along with the gospel. God's way is marvelous. Whenever the gospel was about to reach a certain place, a certain change or action, such as a migration, would occur there.

In the book of Acts, we clearly see a migration taking place. In Jerusalem at the beginning, three thousand people were saved at once, and then at another time, five thousand (2:41; 4:4). In the old days, especially with the inconvenience of transportation, who would be willing to migrate to a faraway place? Most were attached to their native land and were unwilling to leave it. However, with many people saved in Jerusalem and concentrated there, naturally there was no way for the gospel to spread. Therefore, the Lord had to raise up a persecution so that the believers living in Jerusalem were scattered to other localities. These scattered believers went throughout the land preaching the gospel (8:1, 4). When we come to chapter twenty-one of Acts, we see that there was a great number of Christians gathering again at Jerusalem (v. 20). This is a principle: whenever there is a move of the gospel, the residents of the locality involved will have to make a change; that is, a migration has to take place.

THE EXPANSION OF THE GOSPEL IN RECENT TIMES

In Mainland China

The history of China is a history of changes. However, even though there have been many dynastic changes, there have been few changes and movements among the people. It was not until the sixteenth century that the Western wind started to blow toward the East, and the Western culture and customs gradually spread to China. This opened up a way for the gospel. First, Catholic priests such as Matteo Ricci went. Then in the nineteenth century, group after group of Protestant missionaries also went. Once the gospel arrived, China began to change. Later, Dr. Sun Yat-sen, who was influenced by the West, began a revolution. Up until the 1900s, there were still very few believers in China, but due to the Boxer Rebellion, more Western missionaries had the burden to go to China for the gospel. After the establishment of the Chinese Republic, the country was widely opened to the gospel. Because of the changes in the environment, people began to open themselves to changes and would no longer hold on to the old things. By 1920 the gospel invaded the universities, and many young people of high achievements received the Lord.

In Taiwan

Even though this was the case, the gospel was still not prevailing in China. Later, God raised up situations that led to increased and drastic changes. Eventually, several million people left mainland China and settled in Taiwan. We were included in that move. When I first came to Taiwan, I had already been carrying on a work for the Lord for almost twenty years, which was quite fruitful. However, it could not be compared with the work we had after we went to Taiwan. When we first began to work in 1949, people were saved in throngs. This is because the transplanting from mainland China to Taiwan caused the people to become softened in their heart and therefore more ready to receive the gospel.

At that time in Taipei, we had gospel marches every Lord's Day afternoon. After a march, we brought people to the amphitheater at the New Park. The three thousand seats there would be filled each time. After the meeting we would bring back four or five hundred names. The next night we would ask the saints to come together and then distribute the names to them according to districts for follow-up visits one by one. This kind of action proved to be very effective.

People believed in the Lord in groups and companies, and they were caught in "net after net."

Due to the large number of people who received the Lord, I worked out a way to baptize three people in one minute. The plan included seat arrangements, changing into baptismal robes, coming down into the baptistery, being baptized, and changing back into street clothes. I supervised the entire process and especially made sure that each one was baptized in less than twenty seconds. I still remember one baptismal meeting on a Saturday that lasted from 6 P.M. to 9 P.M. Because there were only three hundred eighty baptismal robes, we had to wait until the morning of the following day, which was the Lord's Day, to finish baptizing everyone. That time we baptized more than seven hundred. The saints served by groups in shifts.

The gospel was powerful at that time because the people had experienced a great change. If they had still been in their native land, many of them probably would not have received the gospel. While I was in Chefoo, I had observed and made a study. I found out that Chefoo had a population of about 300,000, less than one-third of which were the local people, the majority being from nearby regions, especially from the Liaotung Peninsula. I myself was not a native of Chefoo; I came from the nearby county of Penglai. Ninety-nine percent of the believers in Chefoo were from other places. Out of one hundred Christians it was hard to find one who was a native of Chefoo. This is because the local people were deeply rooted in their ways. Because they had their families, relatives, neighbors, and family shrines with ancestral tablets, for them to believe in the Lord was extremely difficult.

When I came to Taiwan, after more observations I was finally clear. In the early days in Taiwan, to bring a Taiwanese to believe in the Lord was not easy. To gain a Taiwanese was to gain a treasure. The mainlanders, on the other hand, were considered less valuable because they received the gospel in groups. Sometimes out of three hundred who were baptized, only five or six were natives. Why was this the case? It was because the mainlanders had been uprooted. There is a Chinese saying: "Move a tree and it will die; move a man and he will live." This means that a tree should not be moved, because once it is moved, it may die right away. However, if a man is uprooted and moved, it will be easy for him to live. Therefore, those who migrated to Taiwan from China all survived, and many of them believed in the Lord.

On August 1, 1949, we held a conference and thus officially began our work in Taiwan. At that time the total number of brothers and sisters from the south to the north of the island of Taiwan was no more than three to five hundred. Within five years, however, the number of saints increased to twenty to thirty thousand. At that time none of us thought of going to America. Our heart was to go back to China. We all thought that the Lord's intention was for us to save sinners and nurture the believers in Taiwan; then after a few years, He would bring us back to mainland China as apostles. We could not forget that there were four to five hundred million people waiting for us to preach the gospel for their salvation.

In America

The current of the world never reverses its course or flows backward. Similarly, the flow of the gospel brought us from mainland China to Taiwan and then to America. Ever since my youth, our family had been in contact with some American missionaries, so I understood them very well. A hundred years ago, American missionaries who went to China had to travel by boat for six months. Often they got serious motion sickness. Some died right after they reached the land and were buried there. Some remained in China for at least six to seven years before they could return to their country for a visit. I know much about the hardships they experienced in their labor for the gospel.

In 1938 a saint in Beijing sent me a monetary offering which included two checks—one in the amount of sixteen hundred American dollars and the other in the amount of twelve hundred Chinese yuan. The sender enclosed a letter which read, "Brother Lee, I studied in America. After listening to your preaching of the word, I feel it is truly what America needs. Please go to America! The check for sixteen hundred American dollars is for your round-trip tickets by boat and your living expenses in America. The check for twelve hundred Chinese yuan is for your family. I have calculated that they will need at most one hundred yuan each month, so this money is enough to cover a year's family expenditure." Immediately after I received the letter, I wrote a reply, saying, "I am sorry, but I do not have the interest or the burden to go to America. What should I do with these two checks?" This saint wrote again and said, "Do not return the checks to me. Please keep them. Put them in the bank. I believe that one day the Lord will take you to America."

I deposited the money in the bank. Afterward, because of the change of the political situation in China, the currency changed again and again. In the end, that amount of money was worth only a little. In 1948 some churches in Southeast Asia invited me to visit them. I had just received my passport in Nanking and was about to take the trip, but due to the political situation, our whole family migrated to Taiwan. In Taiwan we did not have the slightest thought of going to the United States. During that time I published a magazine called *The Ministry of the Word,* which contains many messages concerning service. In those messages I often referred to the fact that in bringing us to Taiwan the Lord had put us in a wonderful geographical setting. To the south we could go to Southeast Asia, to the east we could go to Japan and Korea, and at the same time we could take care of mainland China. In Southeast Asia there were a great number of overseas Chinese. As to Japan and Korea, both are very close to the Chinese in culture and writing. In addition, of course, mainland China is a vast land. In those messages I never mentioned anything about the Western world, because I felt that we had no connection with it in terms of culture and language.

Actually, I did not have the intention to labor in Southeast Asia. Since I had been invited, however, I went to the Philippines near the end of 1950. From then on, for about eleven years, I went every year and stayed for at most three or four months each time, mainly in Manila. I did not go to any other places. However, the Lord did not go along with my concept. He stirred up my environment to thrust me to the West.

I came to the United States the first time in 1958. That was because of an invitation which I received from England and Denmark. When I went to Europe, first I stayed in England for a month. Then I went to Denmark and stayed there for about ten days. On my return trip I stopped in America for a short while. Two years later I came to America again; at that time I had a deeper impression. After a year I came to America again, and my impression of it was even deeper. That was twenty-three years ago. There were not many Chinese who went there to study, nor were there many Chinese who immigrated there. At that point I was clear inwardly that I should receive the burden to come and labor in America. Therefore, I applied for immigration. The lawyer told me that America gave the Chinese a quota of only one hundred and five. The Chinese who were already in America had applied for their families to come, and the number of applicants had already exceeded ten thousand. Therefore, if I were to follow the normal procedure, I would have to wait one hundred years for my turn. Fortunately, since I was considered a preacher and because I had written many books, my application was quickly approved.

THE CHINESE-SPEAKING WORK IN AMERICA

Soon after that, Kennedy became the president of the United States. He proposed a revision of the immigration law to remove racial discrimination. Every country would be given a quota of 20,000, but the total number of immigrants could not exceed 300,000 yearly. From the Americas 130,000 would be allowed, while from the other four continents 170,000 would be allowed. The applications would be approved on a first-come, first-served basis. In 1966 Congress passed the new immigration law, and in the next year the implementation of the new law began. From that year on, five countries have met their maximum quota every year; these are China, India, South Korea, the Philippines, and Greece or Italy. Some of the countries did not fill up their quotas, so the Chinese were given more opportunity to come. In addition, a great number of Chinese with special qualifications applied under other categories. Therefore, within seventeen years, there were approximately 500,000 new Chinese immigrants. In 1982 when Reagan became the president, he felt that the Chinese immigrants were performing very well in America, so he gave them special treatment with a double portion— 20,000 for Taiwan and another 20,000 for mainland China. From that time on, there have been 40,000 new Chinese immigrants in America every year. Right now the Chinese make up the largest number of immigrants coming to America per year.

The Chinese immigrants' first choice of residence, which may be related to where their relatives live, is Southern California, and their second choice is New York. Among the new immigrants, many are Christians, including the saints who are in the recovery. Because of this, we have received the burden to start a Chinese-speaking work.

Twenty-three years ago when I received the burden to come to the United States, I was very clear within that the Lord did not want me to work among the Chinese immigrants. Rather, He wanted me to bring His recovery to the typical Americans. Therefore, I concentrated my pioneering work among these Americans. The Lord confirmed this and greatly blessed our work. Beginning in 1970, even though it became evident that we definitely needed a Chinese-speaking work, I still did not touch this matter. This is because I knew that once I gave my attention to the Chinese-speaking work, the English-speaking work would suffer loss. Also, in principle, once the number of the Chinese increases in the meetings, more typical Americans are reluctant to come. Therefore, it was not convenient for me to touch the Chinese-speaking work. In this way, we were not keen in our perception, and after six or seven years we lost from five hundred to one thousand saints. Later we began to have the Chinese-speaking meeting, and two years ago we began the Chinese-speaking work. Now the number of the Chinese saints has become stabilized, and new ones are gradually being gained.

The Language Problem

To summarize the different situations mentioned above, we cannot carry out the Chinese-speaking work in the same way we did two years ago. At that time, I considered that the

Chinese-speaking work was transitory in nature and would serve as a bridge for those with a language problem. Every year forty thousand Chinese have been coming to the United States, and most of them are not proficient in the English language. I studied this situation and felt that if many of the immigrants want to get over the language problem, it would be best if they could come to America under the age of fifteen. If they come after they have graduated from college, they can study, do business, or get a degree, but they will still feel handicapped in the meetings. They cannot thoroughly grasp the meaning of the messages, nor can they freely express themselves in prayer. If after finishing junior high, they come to America to study in high school and college, then after seven years of learning English, they will have just enough to meet the needs of the church life.

We have to admit that language is a problem. If the saints who immigrated here cannot get through this problem within the first three to five years, then it is likely that they will not be able to get through it in their lifetime. They may be able to do grocery shopping, make phone calls, and greet people, but they will not be able to prophesy or pray in the meetings. Therefore, there is a definite need for the Chinese-speaking work. If the Lord allows, I will fellowship with the elders that from now on the Chinese-speaking meeting and work are no longer temporary in nature but are a part of the local church. The American government not only passed the new immigration law but also made preparations to receive the new immigrants by establishing schools and hiring teachers to teach them English. Today the church here cannot be a typical American church; it has to be a local church, a church that includes all the saints in that locality. Since there are many Chinese among the saints, the church will naturally have to make arrangements to include them.

A Biblical Illustration

The book of Acts also shows us a problem with language. In chapter six it says that as the disciples were multiplying in number, the problem of language began to appear. The Hellenists murmured against the Hebrews because their

widows were being overlooked in the daily dispensing. Therefore, the apostles made arrangements for the appointment of
some deacons to take care of the need (vv. 1-6). This indicates
that the church must solve the language problem and meet
the need of all the saints. For the past twenty years, the
Chinese-speaking saints have been somewhat neglected in
America. Therefore, we should now make the proper arrangements for them. That is, the churches should accept the fact
that there should not only be a Chinese-speaking work,
but that such a work should be considered also a part of the
church.

THE TARGETS FOR THE CHINESE-SPEAKING WORK

The Chinese in America can be categorized into two
groups. One group is composed of those who come as foreign
students. Many on the honor rolls in the American schools are
students of Chinese descent. In many of the universities, the
greatest number of foreign students are Chinese. The hearts
of these Chinese students are wide open to the gospel. There
is a university near Dallas that has many Chinese students.
One time, over a hundred of them came to a gospel meeting of
the church, and nearly all of them received the Lord. The
second group is composed of overseas Chinese, including
those in the industrial and business circles. They came to
America to study when they were young, and after they graduated, they stayed to work, spreading in all classes of society.
Because they left their homeland and came to struggle in a
new country, they also are very open to the gospel.

Man is a social being; no man can leave society and live
alone. The best social group is the Christian group, and the
best society is the church. The Chinese left their homeland to
come to America. Since they do not have many relatives or
friends here, they have a great need to belong to a group.
Under this circumstance, to preach the gospel to them will be
very effective. They are Chinese, and we also are Chinese.
Therefore, for us to meet in a foreign land, we naturally feel
very intimate with one another. Moreover, as believers in the
Lord, we are always happy and rejoicing; this invariably stirs
their admiration. Therefore, their hearts have been prepared

by the Lord. Now it depends only on whether or not our spirit is released in our gospel preaching. If we are thick-skinned, open our mouth, and release our spirit, the gospel will enter into people, and they will be saved. The new immigrants are the best targets for our gospel preaching. The older immigrants have become deeply rooted. They have a crowd of relatives and friends, and they are not moved by the gospel. Take Taiwan as an example. Those who migrated to Taiwan from mainland China have already been there thirty years. They have become rooted and have branched out and spread, so it is hard to preach the gospel to them. However, some of them do not intend to stay permanently, and their heart is still soft, so it is still easy to preach the gospel to them. The hardest ones are the local people, the Taiwanese. Their hearts cannot be moved. However, regardless of where the people were originally, once they come to America, they all are immigrants and have all been uprooted, so they are wide open to the gospel.

FULLY COOPERATING
WITH THE LORD'S ARRANGEMENT

I have spoken this much because I hope that you all can see how much the Lord has done in the world situation for the spread of the gospel. Without the Lord's work in the world situation, none of us would have come to America. Nearly none of us had a predetermination to come. Formerly, when I was in mainland China and saw hundreds of churches being raised up, I thought that was truly wonderful. I never even thought about coming to America. Eventually, because the Lord stirred up the environment, we all have come one by one, and more and more are still coming. For this reason we must rise up to face this situation and to cooperate with the Lord's work.

When we began the work in Taiwan, I spoke about a certain principle, and it was printed in *The Ministry of the Word* in 1952. By observing the history of the world, studying the biographies of the saints throughout the ages, and recalling my personal experiences, I saw that wherever the gospel goes, there the Lord's blessing is. Again, take Taiwan as an example. I truly believe that the reason Taiwan is so prosperous today and has become a "miracle" in the world is that the churches with the gospel are there, and therefore the Lord's blessing is also there. However, due to the Lord's blessing people have become rooted again, so the Lord has to stir up the environment once more to uproot them so that all things would work together for the spread of the gospel.

Today the Lord has truly commissioned us with the gospel. Facing this fact, we need to have a response. We need to have people, especially young people, who receive this burden and are led by the Lord to serve full-time. Do not worry that you cannot make a living as a full-timer. Apparently no one takes care of your living, but in actuality the Lord will take care of you. I was saved on a certain afternoon in April 1925. At that time, while I was on my way home, I consecrated myself to the Lord. I determined to give up the world and become a poor preacher going from village to village to preach the gospel for the Lord. If there was no food, I would eat roots from the ground; if there was no water, I would drink water from the mountain. I was prepared to forsake everything and to suffer for the Lord. Those who were my classmates at that time eventually all became successful, but today they have nothing that can compare to what I have. I am living longer than they have, and the money that has passed through my hands is no less than theirs. I did not have to eat roots from the ground, and I did not have to drink water from the mountain. Furthermore, I did not have to walk from village to village; rather, I travel from country to country. This is something that I had never imagined.

Therefore, you young people need not worry. You will not starve serving full-time. You will always have a way to live. Looking back at my own experiences, I cannot explain what happened. To this day the Lord has been leading me. I passed through all kinds of situations and environmental changes, yet I always ended up better than I was before. This is the Lord's doing. Acts chapters twenty-seven and twenty-eight tell us the story of Paul's being delivered as a prisoner on a ship sailing to Rome. Eventually he became the one reigning on the ship. Even the navigator listened to him, and the centurion who put him in chains also listened to him. Whatever he said counted. Even though he was in chains, at the end, he still had the upper hand. This shows us that whoever is for the Lord's gospel will be blessed. Whoever gives himself for the gospel will have the upper hand. Likewise, whoever opposes and tramples the gospel will not have a good ending. History proves this. Therefore, if we live in the world merely to make some money to feed our stomachs, we are not wise.

THE PATTERN OF THE START OF THE WORK IN TAIWAN

Dear saints, we are blessed to be here giving our all for the sake of the gospel. We have to do our best to meet the need of the present situation. When we first arrived in Taiwan, compelled by the situation, we truly gave everything we had. At that time our only thought was that if we die, so be it. We did not care for anything except earnestly preaching the gospel. Whatever number of people there were in Taipei, we would print that many gospel tracts. We asked the brothers and sisters to pass out the tracts within a definite time to every house on the two streets adjacent to the street where they lived. Furthermore, we went to the big streets, small lanes, intersections, and main traffic stations to put up gospel posters with statements such as "Christ Jesus came to the world to save sinners" and "God loves the world." We also had gospel marches on regular days as well as on the Lord's Days. Because the saints were willing to give themselves to the Lord, they were blessed by the Lord even in material things.

As those who are separated by the Lord for Himself, believers cannot love the world. If they love the world, they will suffer. If they do not love the world, they will be blessed. For the gospel's sake, Paul became an ambassador in a chain. While he was held as a prisoner on a ship, the Lord sent an angel to him, who said, "You must stand before Caesar....God has granted you all those who are sailing with you" (Acts 27:24). Thus, Paul became the one who reigned over them. Therefore, Paul was able boldly to say to them, "And now I advise you to cheer up, for there will be no loss of life among you, but only of the ship....For I believe God that it shall be so, even in the way in which it has been spoken to me"

(vv. 22-25). In the end, everything happened according to what Paul had said.

We need to be those who are wise to cooperate with the Lord. If you seek your own success or your own gain, you will not gain what you want. But if you give up the world and give yourself wholly for the Lord and His gospel, the world will be for you. Paul clearly told us that "all things are yours" and "you are Christ's" (1 Cor. 3:21, 23). We believers should clearly see this.

I hope you understand that you did not come to America for your own enjoyment. Rather, you were sent by the Lord to preach the gospel to thousands and thousands of Chinese here in America. You all have to receive this burden. You need to contact them, invite them to your homes, and preach the gospel to them. If all of you would work for the Lord's gospel in one accord, the Lord will give all things and all men to His church, and He will add to us day by day those who are saved.

THE COMMISSION OF THE GOSPEL

(2)

Scripture Reading: Matt. 28:18-19; Mark 16:15; Rom. 1:14-15; 1 Cor. 9:16-17, 22; 2 Tim. 4:2a; Matt. 25:24-30

Hymns, #930 reads as follows:

1 "Must I go, and empty-handed,"
Thus my dear Redeemer meet?
Not one day of service give Him,
Lay no trophy at His feet?

    "Must I go, and empty-handed?"
    Must I meet my Savior so?
    Not one soul with which to greet Him:
    Must I empty-handed go?

2 Not at death I shrink nor falter,
For my Savior saves me now;
But to meet Him empty-handed,
Thought of that now clouds my brow.

3 O the years in sinning wasted;
Could I but recall them now,
I would give them to my Savior,
To His will I'd gladly bow.

4 O ye saints, arouse, be earnest,
Up and work while yet 'tis day;
Ere the night of death o'ertake thee,
Strive for souls while still you may.

This hymn was written long ago in America by Charles C. Luther. It was translated into Chinese at an early date and was widely sung among Chinese Christians. The story behind this hymn concerns an American sister who lived an ordinary Christian life. While she was on her deathbed, she suddenly felt that she had failed the Lord and was ashamed to meet Him because she had not led one person to Him in her lifetime. Therefore, she was exceedingly sorrowful. Her pastor, who was Charles C. Luther, not knowing how to comfort her, wrote this hymn to express her sentiments. When I was young, every time I attended a gospel revival meeting, we would sing this hymn. The tune can easily arouse one's spirit. Even though the original Chinese translation was poor, each time after we sang the hymn, there would always be people walking up to the front in tears and consecrating themselves for the gospel.

Later when I was compiling our hymnal, I spent much time considering whether this particular hymn is suitable to be included. Because our emphasis has always been on such high topics as the Spirit, life, Christ, and the church, I felt that the content and thought of this hymn were rather ordinary and therefore did not deserve to be included. However, because I had obtained a deep impression from this hymn, I truly liked it and could not forget it. Moreover, there is something special about the tune that can easily stir up the believer's spirit for gospel preaching. Therefore, I decided to do my best to improve the translation and to include it in the hymnal.

This hymn says that when a believer dies and goes to meet the Lord, he should not be empty-handed but should offer some trophies to Him. We preach the gospel not in fear of death but because we do not want to meet the Lord empty-handed. That we are saved is not a problem, but we still need to live an overcoming life that we may have trophies to offer to the Lord. Paul said that the believers whom he led to salvation were his hope, joy, and crown of boasting before the Lord (1 Thes. 2:19-20). If when you meet the Lord, you see that everyone else is bringing a herd of lambs and you alone are empty-handed, you will feel sad and ashamed. However, if you also bring with you a good number of lambs, your feeling and joy will be indescribable.

According to this hymn, while we believers are alive, it is day, and when we die, we enter into the dark night, that is, the night of death (stanza 4). We must work while it is day, for when night comes, no one can work (John 9:4). Therefore, while it is still day, before the night falls, we should work actively to save many souls that we may bring with us to offer to the Lord. Although the spiritual meaning of this hymn is not very deep, it has its value in practicality.

SETTLING ACCOUNTS BEFORE THE LORD

While living on earth, we believers should bear fruit and save souls. Then when we meet the Lord or when the Lord comes, we will be able to settle accounts with Him and feel glorious. Otherwise, if we did not lead one person to salvation in our lifetime, we will be full of shame on that day and not have a good feeling.

In Matthew 25:14-30 the Lord Jesus spoke a parable about three slaves. One received five talents, another received two talents, and still another received one talent. The one who received the five talents went and traded with them and gained another five. Similarly, the one who received the two gained another two. But the one who received the one talent felt that he was useless. He did not know how to preach the gospel, how to give a sermon, or how to do any other kind of work. Therefore, in order not to disappoint the Lord or throw away His grace, he dug in the earth and hid his one talent. When the Lord returned, this slave thought he had done a good job because he did not lose the talent but had kept it intact. However, the Lord not only did not praise him but reprimanded him for being an "evil and slothful slave." How strict the Lord is!

The Lord loves us, but sometimes He also rebukes us. If we are not faithful now, when He comes back, He will not let us get away with it; rather, He will rebuke us as being "evil and slothful." The third slave was evil because he had the talent but did not go to work with it, trade with it, or even earn interest with it. Not only so, he blamed the Lord for not sowing or winnowing (Matt. 25:24). To trade with the talent is difficult because it requires psychological as well as physical labor. To earn interest with the talent is also not easy but troublesome because it requires some calculation. However, to wrap the talent in a handkerchief (Luke 19:20) is very easy; it is the slothful way. Therefore, the Lord called that slave an "evil and slothful slave."

The Lord Jesus truly knows the hearts of men, so we all need to be reminded not to be like that slave. He may have thought, "I am not a co-worker or an elder. I cannot do any kind of work. I am slow of tongue and clumsy in utterance. I do not have the talent or the gift of speaking. When I speak, no one listens to me anyway. This is not my fault; the Lord created me this way. Therefore, I have a reason for not working, not preaching the gospel, and not saving souls. The Lord cannot rebuke me." However, the Lord knew his heart and knew that everything he said was an excuse. To put it bluntly, he was lazy.

That slave was not only lazy but also evil. He miscalculated the Lord by making up some excuses, saying, "You created me to be untalented, and You caused me to be born without eloquence. Moreover, You did not give me a good environment to receive a great deal of education. It is already a fortunate thing that I learned enough skill to make a living. But now You are making things difficult for me by asking me to go and lead people to salvation. I do not have this ability. Not only so, Lord, but You seem to be very unreasonable. You asked me to reap where You did not sow; do You expect me to reap from bare land? You also asked me to gather where You did not winnow; are You not imposing a difficult task on me?" He argued at length with perfect assurance.

Nevertheless, the Lord's answer was very remarkable. It seems that He admitted that He is such a Lord who requires His slaves to reap where He did not sow and to gather where He did not winnow. If you ask the Lord, "What do You expect me to reap if You have not sown?" the Lord will answer, "Do not care whether or not I sow. You simply must go and reap. When you go, you will see not only that I sowed but that what I have sown has grown forth." Today you may not see the Lord winnowing, and you may feel that there are no gospel preachers sowing the seed. Accordingly, you may wonder where you can go to reap. In actuality, He has sown much seed, yet you may not know it. He has scattered many seeds, yet you do not see them.

THE LORD ALREADY HAVING DONE THE WORK OF SOWING AND WINNOWING

When we were doing the Chinese-speaking work on American college campuses, we discovered a marvelous thing. It seemed that when we went to reap where there had been no sowing of the seed, there were clusters of fruit. In a Chinese-speaking gospel meeting for new students at the University of Southern California, fifty to sixty people came, and not one rejected the gospel. Who sowed the seed? I can testify that fifty years ago in China, in the early days of my service to the Lord, it was very difficult to preach the gospel to a college student. The college students at that time all thought of themselves as people of the modern age. They idolized science and rejected "superstition," so no one would listen to the gospel. However, under the Lord's sovereign arrangement, after the eight years of the War of Resistance against the Japanese, the situation became completely different. The college students began to be open to the gospel, and there were many who received it. When we resumed our work at that time, I was traveling back and forth between Beijing and Shanghai. One time when we preached the gospel at Chiao Tung University in Shanghai, seven hundred students and professors attended the meeting. The brothers and sisters all wore gospel robes and served in different ways, such as ushering the guests, conducting them to their seats, and conversing with them after the message was given. Over three hundred seventy were baptized. Who did this? It may have seemed to some that the Lord had not sown. Who would ever have thought that He had done much sowing in a hidden way?

When I first came to America, according to my observation the Chinese who came here for advanced studies were very proud, thinking that they were superior to others. When we preached the gospel to them, they would simply ignore us. Nowadays the Chinese who come to America to further their education come in groups and throngs, so they are no longer special, and as a result their attitude is different from that of their predecessors. When we invite them to come and hear the gospel, they come right away. Recently the Chinese-speaking saints in three localities near Dallas preached the gospel. There were a total of one hundred twenty students who came to the three meetings. They were all Chinese. This surely is the Lord's doing.

Therefore, we cannot say to the Lord, "You did not sow, and You did not winnow, so it is unreasonable for You to ask us to reap and gather." Apparently He is not sowing. In actuality we just may not know that He has sown already. Even when He was living on the earth, He said, "Behold, I tell you, Lift up your eyes and look on the fields, for they are already white for harvest" (John 4:35). He then said, "The harvest is great, but the workers few; therefore, beseech the Lord of the harvest that He would thrust out workers into His harvest" (Luke 10:2). This proves that the Lord had already sown the seed which had turned into a harvest that needed workers to reap. Today, this is even more the case.

THE LORD CONTROLLING THE WORLD SITUATION FOR THE SPREADING OF THE GOSPEL

I truly worship the Lord that I have been in His work for more than fifty years. The first thirty years were among the Chinese, so I know very well the situation of the Chinese-speaking work. In America, according to my observation, the atmosphere in the Chinese society and its constituents has completely changed. This is not in the hands of you and me. There is no way we can change the situation. It is the Lord's doing. Therefore, I said in the previous message that based on my observation, my understanding of history, and my fifty years of study of the world situation and the news, I came to a conclusion: Apparently the gospel has nothing to do with the world situation; actually according to history the world situation is all under the control of the Lord's hand with a view for the spreading of the gospel.

Numerous events in history show us clearly that the world situation is in the Lord's hands. He is the Lord of the heavens and the earth, and the throne is His. On the throne He carries out the universal administration and rules over the entire universe. Daniel 2 says, "He deposes kings and causes kings to ascend" (v. 21). We can see in the Old Testament that whatever nation He raised up, that nation would rise; and whatever nation He caused to fall, that nation would fall. What is the purpose of God in governing the universe and ruling over the nations on the earth? We all have to answer that it is fully for the spreading of the gospel.

It was a great event in world history when Columbus sailed the seas and found a new continent. However, very few saw that it was God's doing in order to prepare a place for the gospel to be brought in, on the one hand, and on the other hand, to serve as a refuge that could give protection to the believers who were being persecuted. For several centuries the believers under persecution, such as the Puritans, could not find a safe place to stay in Europe, so they escaped to the new continent. Today we are also refugees. Otherwise, who would be willing to leave their homeland to come to America? Therefore, America is truly a refuge. Thank and praise the Lord that among the six continents there is this piece of land, a land of abundance and freedom, that serves as a shelter to God's children.

America today is not a nation of a single race. Rather, it is a nation made up of "refugees" of many races. The first group that came was the Puritans, who paved the way for the founding of a new nation. The rest of us who came later are the "enjoying refugees." I am a fourth generation Christian. I went with my mother to the Baptist Church when I was little. I was in contact regularly with the Western missionaries, so I liked America from my heart. Nevertheless, I never thought about coming to America. Eventually, however, I came. I truly like America, but I nonetheless miss my homeland. I believe many of you are like this also.

THE LORD'S SOVEREIGN WORK
IN THE MOVES AMONG MANKIND

We have to see that everything on this globe was created by God. We cannot change anything, but the world situation, being under God's sovereign rule, can change. Our move on this earth is not up to us. Today you and I are here in America, but who dreamed about coming here? Nevertheless, we are here. One hundred years ago, to go from America to my homeland Chefoo took up to six months of sailing by boat. To make a round trip would take a year. Many Western missionaries became so sick at sea that they died immediately after landing. However, there were still many more who came in succession. Transportation is much more convenient today. To travel from Shanghai to the west coast of America takes only twelve hours; you can make the round trip in one day. Because of this, the frequency of travel among human communities has greatly increased, and the sphere of travel has also been broadened. Therefore, we have even less excuse for not going out for the gospel.

Even those who were already in America before World War I were not qualified for naturalization, but after the two world wars, the world situation altogether changed. The unequal treaties were revoked automatically, and colonies became independent one after another. As a result, many small countries were raised up. In the United Nations today, all countries both great and small are equal, each having one vote. Facing the international state of affairs, the United States has become lenient concerning the quota of applicants for permanent residence. After 1967 twenty thousand Chinese immigrated here annually. Then since 1982 forty thousand have been coming yearly. For this reason, the Chinese-speaking work has become a task of the greatest urgency at present.

Amazingly, among the saints in the Lord's recovery, those from Taiwan comprise the greatest number, which is almost fifty thousand. Therefore, there are always some saints among the immigrants from Taiwan every year. This forces us to actively carry out the Chinese-speaking work. We work in conjunction with the Lord, and the Lord also works in conjunction with us. Irvine is a newly developed city in Orange County. We foresaw clearly that there should be a church there, so we sent twenty to thirty saints as forerunners. Praise the Lord, after the saints moved to Irvine, the Lord sent multitudes of Chinese there, including many engineers, doctors, and dentists, all of whom are targets for our gospel preaching.

We have to see that it is the Lord who arranges and controls the situation of the whole universe. Revelation, the last book of the Bible, shows us the situation of the churches and of the universe. In chapters four and five, we see that there is a throne in the heavens, and God is sitting upon it. Our Savior, the Lion-Lamb, stands before the throne and receives the scroll to execute God's economy. His seven eyes are the seven Spirits as the executors carrying out His administration. Today the whole world is under the authority of our Redeemer. The unbelievers do not know this, but we know. He is King of kings and Lord of lords (17:14; 19:16). He is above all the kings, rulers, and all those who are in authority. He manages and arranges everything in the universe.

When people are settled, it is not easy to preach the gospel to them. When people move, their hearts turn and become open to the gospel. I saw this in Shanghai and in Chefoo as well. The natives, those who were born and raised there, had a hard time and were afraid to believe in the Lord. The believers were mostly people from out of town. Later, due to circumstances, three million people moved to Taiwan from mainland China all at once. I also went. Preaching the gospel was very easy at that time. A Chinese proverb says, "Move a tree and it will die; move a man and he will live." This has been proven to be true many times in the past. This is why in America the Chinese community, including the Chinese students, are all very open to the gospel. This is because when these Chinese immigrate to a foreign land, they are uprooted, and their hearts begin to turn as well. They have no family relationships here and feel that they are in a strange land. Under these circumstances, when they meet some fellow Chinese who preach the gospel to them, they spontaneously receive it.

We have to understand that the Lord is not only our Redeemer but also the One who arranges the world situation for the spreading of His gospel. Today He has appointed us as His "ambassadors plenipotentiary" to give His gospel to others. The Lord said, "All authority has been given to Me in heaven and on earth. Go therefore and disciple all the nations" (Matt. 28:18-19). Do not think that preaching the gospel is a small matter. We have to see it as a big matter that needs to be carried out through the authority of the heavens and the earth. If there were no operation of the authority of the heavens and the earth, who would listen and believe when we preach the gospel?

BEING VIRGINS WHO FERVENTLY LOVE THE LORD AND SLAVES WHO FAITHFULLY SERVE THE LORD

In six thousand years of human history, no philosophy, doctrine, theory, or any other religion has been so prevailing as the Christian gospel. Today people can talk about and extol many things, but eventually with the passage of time nothing is left. This, however, is not the case with the gospel preached by Christians. Regardless of how people despise, ignore, and oppose the gospel and even attack and persecute the preachers of the gospel, the gospel continues to spread. The gospel will spread throughout the earth and will gain many believers. Many of us can testify that we are not foolish, yet we all heard and believed the gospel and are preaching and speaking Jesus every day.

We not only believe in the Lord but also love Him. In *Hymns*, #208, the first two lines of stanza 2 read, "I love Thee so I know not how / My transports to control." Then stanza 4 reads, "Burn, burn, O love, within my heart, / Burn fiercely night and day, / Till all the dross of earthly loves / Is burned, and burned away." We love the Lord, and we also ask the Lord to burn us; this is to be captivated by the Lord. These words give us a sense of sweetness, though they are not rich in philosophy like, "The principle of the great learning is to cultivate the bright virtue." When I first began to work for the Lord, I was burning with love for the Lord and for the preaching of the gospel. After more than fifty years, the sweetness within is still increasing, and my joy is overflowing. I feel sweet even while I am eating and sleeping. This is the difference between Christians and non-Christians. We do not accept a religion; rather, we believe in the Lord. We are not superstitious; rather, we are enjoying "super-sweetness." The more we believe, the more we feel sweet, and the sweetness becomes so great that we even become "crazy" for Him.

In Matthew 25 the Lord likened His believers to virgins and slaves, indicating that He wants us to be virgins who love Him and slaves who are faithful as He is. He is sowing every day. Only those slaves who are evil and slothful do not see this and say that He wants them to reap where He did not sow. Let us calmly consider how we came to the United States. If it were not for the world situation at present, we would not have come and would not have needed to come. In fact, if it were not for the progress in technology, such as the production of the 747 airplane, we would be bringing misery upon ourselves if we came slowly by boat. Who brought about the intricate situation and the technological progress? The Lord did.

The Lord is not only sovereign over the situations to bring the Chinese to America, but He also opens up their hearts so that the gospel can enter. Many Chinese in America are especially interested in two kinds of business—the restaurant business and the "church" business. In Orange County alone, there are already twenty-nine established Chinese "churches" preaching Jesus Christ. It was not easy to have such a situation thirty years ago, but it is easy now. This is not something you and I could have done; only the Lord can do this.

Therefore, we should not say anymore that the Lord did not sow. Right now the field is ripe, but the workers are few. This requires you and me to rise up to reap the field as His faithful slaves. The Lord Himself does the sowing, but He gives us the job of reaping. When we go out and preach the gospel today, we are not sowing but reaping and gathering.

OUR GOAL BEING TO REAP FOR THE LORD AND NOT TO LIVE FOR OURSELVES

Let us not be so foolish as to believe that the Lord has managed the world situation so that we could come to America merely to live a peaceful life. I appreciate and I like America. Here we have freedom and abundance of material things, and it is not hard to make a living. However, I am also clear that the Lord has sent me here not to enjoy these things but to reap and gather people for Him. I thank the Lord for giving me such great mercy and grace that an old Chinese man such as I, who never studied in America, could be reaping so many Americans here. Now the Lord has committed the Chinese-speaking work to us. This responsibility is not just mine, but it is yours also.

I encourage my grandchildren to study diligently, telling them that this is their responsibility to care for before the age of twenty-five. But I also tell them that regardless of how high an education they receive, their goal should not be their own living in the future but should be the Lord's work. Do not think that the only goal of your coming to America is to make a living, and that you have to struggle very hard to achieve this goal. Actually, America is not so good that if you do not come here, you will not be able to live. If you ask me why I came to America, I would say that I do not know. Nevertheless, the Lord did something and sent me here, so I came with the determination that I am here not merely to live an American life but to gather and reap people for the Lord. This is my greatest joy.

Dear saints, what is the meaning of our human life? What is our goal in coming to America? If we are not here for the preaching of the gospel and saving souls, then what are we here for? You are working so that you can have food to eat, and you have been eating for so many years, yet it is still the same food. What is there to this? If we are not here for the Lord, what is the meaning of our eating? We cannot be the evil and slothful slaves. We must arise to do the work of reaping by actively preaching the gospel.

To the older saints I would say that when you retire, you should not be jobless and stay home. Instead, you should come together in small groups to meet and to pray. Perhaps it is not convenient for you to drive, but you can ask your relatives or friends to help you. Do not feel embarrassed to ask. We never feel embarrassed toward our Lord Jesus. He likes for us to bother Him frequently. If you want your children to take you somewhere merely for your pleasure, that should be condemned. However, since you are going to attend the elderly saints' prayer meeting, it is right to ask your children or grandchildren to serve you. Do not say that you are old and cannot do anything. You are old, but you can still breathe. If you can breathe, then you can pray and preach the gospel. In the same way I would say to the young people that you have to rise up and cooperate. Do not be here merely for making money. Even if you gain the whole of America but do not gain one soul for the Lord, you will have lived and worked your whole life in vain. I hope that you all can see that on that day you will not be able to bring anything before the Lord except souls.

COMING AND GOING

In 1948 I released a message in Shanghai called "Coming and Going." At that time, my burden was very heavy. The Lord said in Matthew 11:28, "Come to Me all who toil and are burdened, and I will give you rest." Then in 28:19 He said, "Go therefore and disciple all the nations." Coming and going is the living the believers should have. We come with sorrow; we go with joy. We come with our sins; we go with grace. We come with death; we go with life. We come empty-handed; we go richly filled with God. Not only so, in coming we are saved; in going we bring others to be saved. Coming, we receive grace; going, we dispense grace to others. Coming, we pour out our pain and sorrow; going, we are filled with joy and peace. This is the normal living of a believer—coming and going.

The Bible speaks more of "going" than of "coming." Regrettably, most of the believers pay attention only to coming, such as coming to be saved, coming to be baptized, coming to the throne of God, coming to the meeting, coming to pray, and coming to read the Word. However, they have neglected the matter of going, such as, "Go therefore and disciple all the nations" (Matt. 28:19); "Go into all the world and proclaim the gospel" (Mark 16:15); and "Go; behold, I send you" (Luke 10:3). In Isaiah 6 the Lord said, "Whom shall I send? Who will go for Us?" (v. 8). This indicates that almost no one is willing to go for the Lord. The believers who can and will come are few; those who will go and who can be useful are even fewer. Hence, we need to be reminded not to be a "half believer" but to be a "whole believer"; that is, not to be a "coming yet not going" believer but a "coming and going" believer.

THE BIG REVIVAL IN CHEFOO
AND THE UNDERTAKING OF MIGRATION

There was a background to my speaking in 1948 concerning coming and going. In 1943 there was a big revival in Chefoo. It is hard to describe the condition of that revival. I can still remember a sister here in Anaheim who was saved in that revival. When she first came among us, I saw that her hair was like a tower of three stories. I could see it clearly from the platform. There were several hundred people in the room, but only this young lady's hair was "three stories" high. However, one day when she came again, the top story was gone. After a few days the second story was also gone, and not long afterward her hair became even. During this time she was saved.

There was a brother named Sun Fung-lu, who was a judge at the local court. He loved the Lord very much after his salvation. Later, he became one of the elders in the church in Taipei. During the Chefoo revival, he had just been promoted from a local court to the higher court. One day he came to me and said that the condition of the Chefoo revival was probably more glorious than the condition portrayed in the Acts and that it was worthwhile to record it as history. In truth this might not have been so, but the impact of that revival was far beyond one's imagination.

I can still remember the current of the revival. It began from December 31, 1942. The afternoon after the Lord's Day meeting an announcement was made that there would be a meeting on the next day. What followed was one hundred continuous days of meetings. The time was not scheduled, but it was from morning to night. There was also no specific procedure for the meeting; everyone was free in spirit. Mostly it was I who gave the messages, but there was not a particular subject. The meetings were different every day. The Spirit truly was free. Hence, it can be said that it was a real revival.

After a month, on a Lord's Day afternoon, we blessed the saints by laying hands on them. The elders and I knelt down in the center of the meeting hall and laid our hands on the heads of the saints. The saints, brothers and sisters separately, knelt down in the two aisles. They came forth one by one to receive the laying on of hands. You could not imagine it. The prayers for that many saints were just one continual prayer when put together, even though the portion that each saint received was fitting to his situation. It was the work of the Spirit. Included in that prayer were many biblical allusions such as "You are a little Benjamin," and "You are John." We laid our hands on and prayed for over two hundred saints. Afterward, everyone rose and was surprised at how marvelous that prayer had been. Later on, those who had received the laying on of hands testified that the words of blessing were exactly fitting for each of them.

On another Lord's Day, after the preaching of the gospel in the morning, there was an edification meeting in the afternoon. Before I was about to release the message, I had a feeling within that I needed to pray, so I did. Once I opened my mouth and began to pray, I could not stop. I raised my left hand and prayed loudly that the Lord would shake us. Saints later testified that this prayer was like a waterfall pouring down. After I prayed with my hand lifted for half an hour, a brother came up to the platform to support my arm. I was there praying, and he was there supporting. That occasion was truly amazing.

This revival brought forth a great undertaking of migration. The first group to go comprised seventy saints. They each consecrated their whole family and set out in April of 1943. They sailed from Tientsin and then moved on to Suiyuan Province in Inner Mongolia. Their boat tickets were bought with the money offered to the church; we also provided each one with three months of living expenses. Originally, a number of Swedish and British missionaries from the China Inland Mission had been working in the region of Suiyuan for many years. However, due to the breaking out of the Pacific War, all the Caucasians, including the missionaries, had been imprisoned. The saints who migrated there were engaged in shoe repair, teaching, selling goods, and other trades. Their zeal for the gospel and their one accord truly touched the local Christians, who subsequently came and joined them. By the end of 1943 more than forty churches had been raised up.

Another thirty saints went out at the same time with the

first wave. They set out from Chefoo to the mouth of the Yalu River in Antung Province, in the northeast of China. Thus, at one time there were one hundred saints who migrated from Chefoo. This move shocked the office of the Japanese secret agents. They could not understand what had happened that such a small civic organization had such a great mobilizing power. They therefore put me into prison and interrogated me with severe torture for a month. After they concluded that I was just a "Jesus addict" who was leading a group of other "Jesus addicts" to do such things, they released me.

FROM HOUSE TO HOUSE

Dear brothers and sisters, we do not need to migrate to Suiyuan or Antung. We simply need to go to the places close to where we live; that is enough. The Lord has already delivered the crops to our door and driven the fish into our water. If we would just give this matter a little attention and exert a little energy, we will be able to gain many Chinese around us, gathering them into our nets and putting them into our storehouses. Now it simply depends on whether or not we will cooperate with the Lord as His good slaves to open our homes to reap and to gather His crops.

The book of Acts shows us that once a church was established, the saints began to preach the gospel and to meet from house to house. Verses 46 and 47 of chapter two speak of the saints' breaking bread from "house to house" and having grace with all the people, and the Lord adding together day by day those who were being saved. Verse 42 of chapter five says that every day, "from house to house, they [the saints] did not cease teaching and announcing the gospel of Jesus as the Christ." As we follow their pattern to open our houses, we do not need to find those who are far away. We only have to invite the ones in our neighborhood to come to our house. Do not say that you cannot do it. You cannot because you will not. As soon as you will, the gospel can spontaneously go out.

When the faucet is turned on, more water will come; if you do not let the water go out, no more water will come. Therefore, coming is the effect of going. As long as the water keeps flowing out, the water from the source will keep flowing in.

You came because of the Lord's grace, but if you do not flow out, grace also will stop flowing. Therefore, do not think that you cannot speak; even if you truly do not know how to speak, do not worry. Simply open your doors to invite three or five, or eight or ten, of your neighbors to come for a meal, tea, or a brief conversation. Just tell them that you are a Christian and that you would like to share grace with them. Then you can give them your testimony and lead them to sing a hymn. Once you open your doors and invite people in, once you open your mouth to release what is within you, the Lord will bless and add some saved ones to the church.

To do this will easily bring in people. It is easier than dragging people to the meetings. It is hard not to have a form in a meeting, and once there is a form, people become uncomfortable and uneasy. But if you invite people into your homes to have tea and to talk, they will spontaneously be open. If we do this often, the blessing will pour in like great waters. I believe that after half a year you will see sprouts everywhere. Soon there will be a harvest, and the number of people will more than double.

A CONCLUDING WORD

By observing the situation, you can all see the work of the Lord. When the Chinese come to this country, they feel that they are foreigners. They see Americans all around them, and it is hard for them not to feel alienated. Since you are also Chinese, if you go and pay them a visit to sit in their homes and to warm their hearts, they will be touched. Then you can invite them to your homes and have some association with them. In this way you will surely touch their hearts. Human beings are neither wood nor stones. It takes only a few contacts to move a person. Once he is moved, it is easy to preach the gospel to him.

At the same time, we need to be bold. We are not leading others to go downhill; rather, we are leading them to go upward—to fear God, to worship God, and to believe in the Lord. This is truly the right path. Moreover, our Lord is living. As the Spirit, He is with us and works with us. He blesses and works along with us. Therefore, all that is needed is that we

take action. This action is what the Bible refers to as "going."
You need to go!

According to history, America is really the "uttermost part
of the earth." Whether we came as immigrants or refugees, we
have all come to the "uttermost part of the earth." We do not
need to exert much energy. We simply need to open the door of
our houses to welcome people and sit down with them to talk,
sing hymns, and preach the gospel. I believe many will be
reaped in. This will be our glory and our crown. Paul said that
he was a debtor to all men (Rom. 1:14). I hope that we will
have the same spirit to see that we are those who owe the
debt of the gospel. Paul also said that it would be woe to him
if he did not preach the gospel, but if he preached the gospel,
he would be rewarded (1 Cor. 9:16-17). I hope that we will all
rise up to be the Lord's witnesses that we may be rewarded
for the gospel.

CHAPTER THREE

THE POWER OF THE GOSPEL

Scripture Reading: Luke 24:47-49; Acts 1:8, 14; 4:8; 13:9; 6:4, 7; 12:24; 19:20; Rom. 1:16

THE POWER OF THE GOSPEL
BEING THE POURED OUT SPIRIT

In the last two chapters we saw the commission of the gospel. In this chapter, we will go on to see the power of the gospel. God not only has given us a commission to preach His gospel; He has also given us power to accomplish the commission He has given us. The New Testament reveals that the Lord sends us to preach the gospel, as those who go to do business. Since this is the case, the Lord has to give us the capital, and this capital is our power. Therefore, the Lord not only has commissioned us with the gospel, charging us to preach it; He has also given us the power that enables us to preach the gospel.

In Luke 24:47 the Lord charged the disciples to go "that repentance for forgiveness of sins would be proclaimed in His name to all the nations, beginning from Jerusalem." This is very similar to the word in the Gospels of Matthew and Mark. Matthew 28:19 says, "Go therefore and disciple all the nations." This indicates that the authority the Lord received was for His disciples to go and disciple all the nations. Mark 16:15 says, "Go into all the world and proclaim the gospel to all the creation." These three verses indicate that the believers have been sent to preach the Lord's gospel. However, if we do not read carefully, we will not see that within this charge there is a support, which is the power of the Lord.

Matthew 28:18 says, "All authority has been given to Me

in heaven and on earth." The Lord's authority is mentioned here, but how this authority is related to the disciples is not mentioned. It is in Luke 24:49 that the Lord charged the disciples, "And behold, I send forth the promise of My Father upon you; but as for you, stay in the city until you put on power from on high." This means that the disciples had not yet received the power as their capital. Therefore, they had to stay and wait in Jerusalem and not go anywhere else. The Lord sent the disciples to go and do business, so they had to wait for the Lord to give them their capital, that is, to pour down what had been promised by the Father. This was to be the power of the gospel.

This power includes the Triune God—the Son as the Pourer poured out the Spirit promised by the Father. The Father promised, the Son poured, and the Spirit was poured out. This promise that was in the Old Testament in Joel (2:28-32) was fulfilled in Acts 2. In Acts 1 the Lord said that in His ascension He would fulfill what the Father had promised by pouring down the Spirit of power. When the disciples received this power, they would start from Jerusalem, go on into Judea and Samaria, and then go unto the uttermost part of the earth (vv. 4-5, 8).

When the Holy Spirit descended, the disciples were filled with the Spirit outwardly. They were like those who were filled with new wine and all became "crazy." When others saw them and said, "They are full of new wine!" (2:13), Peter and the eleven disciples stood up and said that they were not drunk but that they had the Spirit who was poured upon them. Then they began to preach the gospel, and as a result, three thousand were saved.

A HISTORY OF THE OUTPOURING OF THE HOLY SPIRIT

Two centuries ago, the truth concerning the outpouring of the Holy Spirit was neglected by organized, formal Christianity in its degradation. The result was a lack of attention to this truth by Christians. For this reason, two hundred years ago almost no one talked about the outpouring of the Holy Spirit. Nonetheless, in church history there have always been believers who experienced the power of the outpouring of the Holy Spirit.

THE RISE OF THE MYSTICS

In my study of church history and the biographies of earlier saints, I discovered that after the Reformation with Martin Luther, the Catholic Church remained apostate and dead, while the Protestant churches eventually became dry and weak. It was in such a situation of dryness and deadness that God raised up the so-called inner-life people, the mystics. Madame Guyon was one of these. Their sole emphasis was on how to experience the Lord inwardly and take Him as life. However, because of their neglect of the work of the Holy Spirit, there was no spread of the gospel.

The Moravian Brethren

In the same period as the inner-life seekers, God raised up the "brethren" in Bohemia. (The Puritans, who are well known in history, were influenced by them.) They devoted themselves exclusively to studying the Scriptures, neither following the Catholic dogma nor caring for established practices. Consequently, because they were oppressed by the Catholic Church and rejected by the other established churches, they fled to Moravia. Later, in the eighteenth century, Count Zinzendorf of Saxony, North Germany, was touched by the situation of the descendants of these brethren, and he received them, providing them a place of refuge on his estate. These believers were determined to recover the testimony of the church that their families of old had previously had in Bohemia. This latter group was called the Moravian Brethren.

Later, those who loved the Lord with a pure heart gradually came from different places to join them. Then they began to have disagreements among themselves and were constantly engaged in debates concerning doctrines and practices. One day Zinzendorf asked the leaders of the different groups to come together, and he exhorted them to discontinue their arguments over trivial matters and to turn their attention to the crucial matters such as experiencing the Lord and receiving the Spirit. Those brothers were moved, and they

agreed to everything Zinzendorf said. They signed an agreement to immediately stop any unnecessary arguments and to
practice being in one accord. When the next Lord's Day came,
while they were breaking bread in one accord to remember
the Lord, they experienced the outpouring of the Holy Spirit
and all became "crazy." However, there is no record in history
telling us that they spoke in tongues, cast out demons, and
healed the sick. Rather, there are clear records telling us that
they were filled with the Holy Spirit outwardly—that is, they
received the outpouring of the Holy Spirit—and consequently
they consecrated themselves and all they had to the Lord and
also prepared themselves to migrate to other countries for the
preaching of the gospel.

That was already two hundred years after the discovery of
the new continent. Many of the Puritans had migrated to the
new continent from Europe to escape persecution. A good
number of the Moravian Brethren also moved there, and they
greatly affected the spiritual condition of the Puritans in
America. Furthermore, John Wesley, who was raised up
around that time in England, was invited to come to preach in
America and was on the same boat as a group of Moravian
brethren. When the boat encountered a storm on the sea,
almost everyone on board was exceedingly fearful. Wesley
saw a group of people who were not afraid at all; instead, they
sang and prayed calmly in a corner. Greatly impressed, he
went over and joined their fellowship. It was then that
he found out they were Moravian Brethren.

The Revival in England

Upon returning to England, John Wesley became a powerful evangelist. He rejected all the things of the Catholic
Church and renounced the practices of the state Church of
England as well. He did not preach in church buildings or in
the sanctuaries of the Church of England. Rather, he
preached the gospel on the streets to the coal miners. I once
saw a picture of people with black faces but with two white
lines running down from their eyes. They were miners who
had just come out of the coal pits. They heard John Wesley's

preaching and could not help shedding tears, producing two white lines on their black faces. It was truly touching. From that time on, Christians in England were no longer bound by the old religion. While John Wesley was preaching, some were crying while others were laughing. Their shouts of "Amen!" reverberated through the sky. Later on, this practice spread to America. However, some people could not tolerate this, so an "Amen Corner" was reserved in the Wesleyan chapels for the "Amen shouters." The Quakers were influenced by them. The founder, Mr. George Fox, shook whenever he gave a sermon. In Taiwan there is a chair-shaking group. This proves the great influence that John Wesley had on England and Christianity.

Not only so, the upheaval of the French Revolution in 1789 spread through continental Europe. England was also affected by this revolutionary storm. However, because of John Wesley's great evangelistic power, the storm was calmed down, and the effect of the French Revolution on England was annulled. Because the royal family was very grateful for this, Wesley is commemorated at Westminster Abbey, thereby affirming his contribution to England.

The Rise of the Pentecostal Movement

Due to the influence of John Wesley and George Fox, the Pentecostal movement quickly sprang up. This movement was mainly to break through the old rules and to use the way of shouting to be released. Compared to the early days, the present Pentecostal movement is more orderly. Once Brother Nee and I went to a Pentecostal meeting. We saw that some of them were jumping, some were shouting, some were yelling, some were laughing, and some were rolling. Each one did as he preferred without caring for others. When the pastor was about to speak, no one paid attention to him. It was not until the pastor beat a gong a few times that the congregation calmed down. After the meeting, I was walking home together with Brother Nee, and I said to him, "What way of meeting was that, with shouting, jumping, and rolling?" Brother Nee's response shocked me. He said the New Testament does not have rules telling us how to have a meeting.

God's Reaction

Now fifty years have passed. These movements, from the mystics to the Pentecostals, were all originally reactions by God. Because the church did not pay attention to the Holy Spirit, these reactions came forth. However, these reactions went overboard, eventually producing the Pentecostal movement with shouting, speaking in tongues, interpreting of tongues, predicting, healing, and casting out of demons. I have seen all of these things. Because many of these practices were false, people gradually stopped believing in them. Nonetheless, this was originally God's reaction with the intent that His children would rise up and pay attention to the power of the Holy Spirit.

THE HISTORY OF THE HOLY SPIRIT

The Third of the Divine Trinity

What is the power of the gospel? The power of the gospel is the Holy Spirit. I am concerned that even the saints in the Lord's recovery have not paid adequate attention to the Holy Spirit. Doctrinally, the Holy Spirit is a mystery, just as the Triune God is a mystery. Simply speaking, the Holy Spirit is the third of the Divine Trinity and the ultimate expression of the Triune God. We cannot thoroughly explain the Triune God. He is not the Father apart from the Son; nor is He the Son apart from the Father and the Spirit. This is the wrong traditional doctrine taught in Christianity. According to the Bible, the three of the Triune God are always together.

The Lord's speaking in Luke 24:49 indicates that the Son would pour out the Holy Spirit as the promise of the Father. When we read the Bible, we often accept everything as a matter of course and therefore do not study to find the reasons behind it. This verse reveals that the Father promised and that the Son poured out. Since the Father could make the promise, could He not also do the pouring out? Since the Son could do the pouring out, could He not also make the promise? Of course, They could do so. This simply shows that the One who promised and the One who poured out are actually the same person, yet with a distinction. The Father promised, and the Son poured out what was promised. According to Acts 1:8, what the Son poured out was the Spirit. However, Luke 24:49 tells us only that what would be sent forth, or poured out, was power and that this power was to be put on as a mantle by the disciples. According to the utterance, it seems there are three: the Father who promised, the Son who poured out, and the Spirit who descended. Actually, They are not merely three but triune: the One who promised was the One who poured out, and the One who poured out was the One who descended. The three are one. Therefore, the Spirit as the descending One is the Triune God.

The Ultimate Consummation of the Triune God

Before incarnation, the Triune God did not pass through any processes. In eternity past, He created the universe without going through a process. He spoke, and it was; He commanded, and it stood (Psa. 33:9). He said, "Let there be light; and there was light" (Gen. 1:3). He said there were to be the heavens and the earth, and the heavens and the earth were produced. It was not until two thousand years ago when He became flesh that the Triune God began to go through various processes. He first entered into the womb of the virgin Mary where He was conceived, and then He was born as "the holy thing" (Luke 1:35). In the past, we may have thought that the One who became flesh was only the Son. However, Isaiah 9:6 clearly says that the child born in the manger was the "Mighty God," the Triune God. This is the first process the Triune God went through.

Since God is almighty and whatever He says comes into being, why did He not become a man instantly? Instead, He came to be in the womb of a virgin for nine months and then was born. Then He grew from a babe to become an adult, just like any normal human being. Moreover, the process of His growing up was not simple. For thirty years He did carpentry in a poor carpenter's home. The foolish Jews thought that God was in the temple, so they went there to worship and serve God by burning incense and offering sacrifices. Actually, God was not in the temple; He was a carpenter in Nazareth. The almighty God became a lowly carpenter named Jesus.

This was hard for the Jews to believe, and they were stumbled by it.

At the age of thirty, as the Lord Jesus began to minister, the Spirit of God descended upon Him to be His power economically. As the Triune God He already had the Holy Spirit within Him. However, for His ministry, His work, He still needed the Spirit to descend upon Him as His power. In His three and a half years of ministry, He lived an extraordinary life in which God was expressed. Afterward, He was crucified on the cross, entered into the tomb, and descended into Hades. He stayed there for three days and accomplished something further, and then He came out in resurrection. The Bible tells us that in His resurrection, the last Adam, the lowly carpenter, became the life-giving Spirit (1 Cor. 15:45b). Therefore, on the night of His resurrection, when He came to the disciples, He was actually the Spirit. In Greek, *Spirit* and *breath* are the same word—*pneuma*. When the Lord breathed into the disciples, He was actually breathing Himself as the Spirit of reality into them.

Afterward, He spent forty days to train the disciples to live by this wonderful and mysterious One and to practice His invisible presence. It was hard for the disciples to see Him come and go and not know what was happening. Actually, His going was His coming, and His coming was His going. He was with the disciples in a hidden way. When there was the need, He would reveal Himself to them. This was to train them to realize His invisible presence. After forty days, He told the disciples "not to depart from Jerusalem, but to wait for the promise of the Father, which, He said, You heard from Me" (Acts 1:4). He then ascended to the heavens from the Mount of Olives before their eyes.

According to the Lord's word, the disciples waited and prayed for ten days, after which the Holy Spirit was poured out upon them. Who was this Holy Spirit? He was the ultimate consummation of the Triune God. At this point the Triune God was no longer simple. Thirty years before, He was only God; He did not have humanity. He had not entered into the womb of a virgin, and He had not become flesh. Moreover, He had not passed through the processes of death, resurrection, and ascension. Now, however, the Triune God is different. He has divinity with humanity, and He has passed through death and resurrection, entered into ascension, and descended. He passed through a complete process to become the ultimate expression of the Triune God.

What we received when we were saved was this Spirit. He is the Spirit of life within us for our living. He is also the Spirit of power upon us for our work. According to the truth, on the night of the Lord's resurrection the Spirit of life was breathed into the believers as breath (John 20:22). Fifty days later, on the day of Pentecost, the Spirit of power descended like a great wind upon the believers. Now both matters have been accomplished and have become history. It is at this point that Peter spoke with reference to Joel that everyone who calls on the name of the Lord shall be saved (Acts 2:21). Therefore, God had to pass through the necessary processes in order to pour Himself down so that when men call on the Lord's name, they can be saved. If God had not been processed to such an extent, it would not be possible for man to be saved.

TO BE SAVED BEING TO RECEIVE THE HOLY SPIRIT IN TWO ASPECTS

Now we want to see what it is to be saved. To be saved ultimately is to receive the Spirit. On the day of Pentecost, those who were touched by Peter's preaching asked, "What should we do?" Peter said, "Repent and...be baptized...for the forgiveness of your sins, and you will receive the gift of the Holy Spirit" (Acts 2:37-38). Repent, be baptized, and receive the Holy Spirit—this is to be saved. The Holy Spirit we received through salvation is the Triune God. He is to be not only our life but also our power.

Doctrinally, there are two aspects to our receiving of the Spirit. Experientially, however, the two aspects are not in sequence. That a person is saved does not mean that he first has the experience of John 20 to receive the Spirit of life breathed into him and then has to wait for another day to have the Spirit of power descend upon him. In doctrine, this is a sequence of two steps, but today in our experience it is not as complicated. This is because the Spirit is a complete Spirit—He is the Spirit of life and also the Spirit of power. When we believe in the Lord and call on His name, immediately we are saved, and the Lord as the Spirit comes into us to be our life and also descends upon us to be our power.

THE WIND, THE CLOUD, THE FIRE, AND THE ELECTRUM

The chorus of the Chinese *Hymns,* #212 says,

Blowing! Blowing! The Holy Spirit, the great wind, blowing!
Covering! Covering! The Spirit, the great cloud, covering!
Burning! Burning! The holy fire burning!
Glowing! Glowing! God's electrum glowing!

The wind, the cloud, the fire, and the electrum are the content of chapter one of Ezekiel. In 1961 I had a study with the church in Taipei on the book of Ezekiel. I gave many messages just on chapter one alone. Ezekiel begins with a storm wind from the north (God's dwelling place). The wind brings a great cloud, and as the cloud covers, the fire begins to burn. Then once the fire burns, the electrum begins to appear. This section of the Old Testament is a prophecy with a type. The Spirit we have received today is a great wind, a great cloud, and a great fire, and within there is also the electrum. He is the wind, the cloud, the fire, and the electrum.

Therefore, when we receive the Spirit today, we become people who are always of wind, cloud, and fire. These three things—wind, cloud, and fire—are constantly creating events in the universe. Whenever wind and clouds are stirred up in the world's political situation, war breaks out and fire begins to burn. However, the fire's burning always brings out something good—the electrum. Therefore, do not be afraid of war. History proves that whenever there is war, the electrum is produced. This is the doing of the Lord Jesus. When the situation is suitable and the opportunity comes, He will blow the wind from the throne. When the wind blows, the cloud follows. Then there is shaking in the world situation: war breaks out and fire is burning everywhere. After the burning, the electrum is produced. This is what is meant by the Chinese proverb: "When the snipe and the clam fight, they both become captives of the fisherman." The Lord Jesus is the "fisherman" who "captures" much electrum as a result of wars.

In 1950 the church in Hong Kong was considering to buy a piece of land in Tsim Sha Tsui to build a meeting hall. At that time, Brother Watchman Nee first helped to form a group to carry out acquisition and construction and then charged the brothers, saying, "Whatever Brother Witness tells you concerning the land, listen to him and quickly buy it." The brothers then took me to see the land. At that time it was still a vegetable garden. When I saw it, I said that Tsim Sha Tsui would become the center of Hong Kong and Kowloon because it is conveniently located near the ferry. Therefore, we bought the land in a short time. It was just as I had predicted. When the brothers asked me how much land they should buy, I said they should buy at least twelve thousand square feet. The brothers lost faith when they heard this, because the total cost of the land was approximately fifty thousand U. S. dollars. That amount is insignificant at the present time, but at that time it was exceedingly high. Because of this, they asked me if they could reduce the purchase by one-half. I laughed and said, "This is your business; do not ask me for a reduction. Still, I have to say that if you do not buy it now, you will regret it later, and when you do want to buy it, you will not be able to." They thought they had my approval, so they went and bought six thousand square feet. Once they started to build, however, they realized that they had bought too small a portion of land. Therefore, they went back to buy more but were able to buy only another three thousand square feet.

I relate this story to illustrate that the world situation is ever changing to produce the electrum. However, the Lord will not gather the electrum Himself. He wants us to do it. If we hesitate and delay, we will suffer loss. We have been "blown" to America by the great wind. Some may have thought that they came just to study for a degree or to make a business investment. It never occurred to them that they would settle here permanently. This was their view; it was not the Lord's view. He sent us here by the wind and carried us here by the cloud. He did this so that we could preach the gospel here to gain the electrum!

ENJOYING THE ALL-INCLUSIVE SPIRIT AS OUR POWER

Let us not listen to what Christianity teaches nor care for what Pentecostalism practices. We need to come back to the Bible itself. The New Testament clearly reveals that this One who became flesh, passed through human living, entered into death, was buried, resurrected, ascended, descended, and became the life-giving Spirit is the mysterious and marvelous One. He is our Lord, our God, our Redeemer, and our Savior. Moreover, He is the Spirit of life and the Spirit of power. He is the wonderful One.

Today the electrum is in the Spirit, and the Lord is this Spirit. This Spirit passed through the breathing in John 20 and the blowing in Acts 2 to be the complete Spirit with both divinity and humanity. Today you and I are saved; we have received the complete Spirit. There is no need for us to experience the process of the breathing and the blowing. However, the problem lies in that even though we have the Spirit, we may not enjoy or experience Him. Children who are foolish and lazy do not eat good food when it is available and do not put on good shoes when they have them. What we have received today is the all-inclusive Spirit. He has immeasurable riches, so we must enjoy Him.

RECEIVING THE POWER OF THE GOSPEL

Our power for the preaching of the gospel depends on our enjoyment of this all-inclusive Spirit. We all know that before we preach the gospel, we should pray to contact God and to enjoy Him. This is to "wait." By praying and waiting we enjoy God. Then when we go out, we have the power of the gospel. On the other hand, we also need to learn and understand the truths. Peter said in Acts 6:4, "We will continue steadfastly in prayer and in the ministry of the word." To pray is to contact God, and to be in the ministry of the word is to release the Lord's gospel to others. When the apostles did this, the result was that the word of the Lord grew, multiplied, and prevailed (v. 7; 12:24; 19:20).

In order to receive the power of the gospel, we have to enjoy the Lord. Once we enjoy the Lord, the Lord becomes breath and a storm wind to us. The storm wind brings the great cloud, and the great cloud brings the consuming fire. This is power. The wind, the cloud, and the fire are the power in the universe, and the issue is the electrum. Not only so, we also need to speak the truth of the gospel. When we open our homes and invite people to come, we cannot be silent. Rather, we have to speak boldly. We may not understand technology, astronomy, or geography, but we know the gospel and are clear about the biblical truths. This is enough; we need to spread the Lord's word to others.

Therefore, dear saints, the power of the gospel is in these three things: God Himself as the consummated Spirit, our prayer, and our preaching of His word. God is the Spirit of life and of power, and the Spirit is in us as our life and upon us as our power. When we enjoy Him, wait on Him, pray to Him, and learn His word, we receive power. The result is that electrum is produced.

However, we should not forget that the gospel is "the power of God unto salvation to every one who believes" (Rom. 1:16). The gospel is the word of God with God Himself becoming our power through our enjoyment and prayer. Before we open our homes to receive guests, we need to enjoy God in His word and receive power. We need to have the capital before we do the business. When we pray to Him and wait on Him, the wind will start to blow, the cloud with the fire will come, and the electrum will be produced.

HOW TO "DO BUSINESS"

When we came to Anaheim ten years ago, there were not many Chinese here. Up until three or four years ago, the Chinese population had increased to more than ten thousand. Now it has even doubled. Recently the newspaper reported that the largest number of Chinese in California is in San Francisco; the second largest is in Los Angeles, and the third largest is in Orange County. Among these three, Orange County is the highest newly developed area, and the church in Anaheim is located in the center of Orange County. Thank the Lord for giving us this land for us to build the big meeting hall. Now we must receive the burden to actively do the Chinese-speaking work and to fill this big meeting hall.

Dear brothers and sisters, our Lord is the Lord of lords and King of kings. He changed the world situation and rearranged everything not for America and not for China but for His own gospel. Many who do not believe in the Lord have been blown by the wind to America without understanding why. They do not realize that if they had stayed in their homeland, they would be worshipping idols and would not be able to believe in the Lord by any means, and that because of this, the Lord blew them here to give them this opportunity to receive the Lord. When the wind blows, the heart is moved. Not only did they come to America, but many have been willing even to come to our meeting hall. Now we have gospel candidates, and we also have the meeting hall. The question is whether or not we will receive the burden to open our homes for the work of the gospel.

At Corinth, two to three years before Paul went to Rome, he wrote the book of Romans to the church in Rome. This must have touched and benefited the saints in Rome. Therefore, in Acts 28 when he and his companions came to the Market of Appius and Three Inns, the brothers in Rome came to meet them (v. 15). Rome is about forty miles from the Market of Appius and thirty from Three Inns. The transportation in the ancient days was not convenient, but the saints still paid the price to host them. Today the Lord does not ask us to pay a big price. He has already blown the Chinese to our front door and has prepared the meeting hall. We should cooperate by consecrating our homes and our time so that our homes can each become the Market of Appius and Three Inns. At Paul's time there was only "Three Inns"; today we should have "One Hundred Inns."

I hope that you will make a solemn decision before the Lord today to reconsecrate yourself for the move of His gospel and to consecrate your time to the best of your ability for His gospel. Then open your house to make it a gospel station. We all are weak and need the help of a binding consecration. Even when the people of the world discuss business, nothing is accomplished if no decision is made at the end. Today we cannot merely listen to the gospel and be excited for a while. We have to make an agreement before the Lord by consecrating ourselves to Him in a practical way.

This is our responsibility, and it is also our opportunity. Our advancement on this earth and all the material wealth we have received will become vanity in the end. Only the souls we have gained for our Lord will have real value and will last until eternity. Therefore, saints, do not be afraid that you will not have food to eat. The more you are for the Lord and for His gospel, the better your food will be. I myself have countless testimonies in this matter. Fifty years ago there was a saying in Chinese that if a person becomes a preacher, he will live a simple life in poverty. On the day I was saved, I was clear that I had been called by the Lord. I was determined that if I were to be poor, so be it, but I would still preach the gospel for Him. Eventually, in these fifty years the Lord has not made me poor. On the contrary, the food He provides has been better and better. My former classmates all thought that I was superstitious, but later on, one by one they were convinced that the more I served the Lord, the more blessed I was.

To the young people I would say that you should not be afraid. Right now it seems to not be easy, but ultimately you will be blessed by the Lord. If a person is not for the Lord and for His gospel, he will have many misfortunes. I am not speaking a curse, nor am I advising you not to study and work. I simply want you to be clear that the Lord has blown us here not so that we can live here in peace, having a good job and sleeping well. His goal is that we save souls to offer to Him for His building. I hope that you all will see this clearly and will truly consecrate yourself and your time for the Lord's gospel.

Prayer: Lord, thank You that You have opened our eyes. We truly understand the world situation. We have seen Your doings, we have clearly recognized the way, and we have found the direction. Lord, it is You who have brought us here for Your gospel. You have prepared everything for us so that we have no lack in anything; we are abundantly rich. We do not want to be foolish, we do not want to be blind, and we do not want to fail You. We consecrate ourselves wholly for You, and we consecrate our time, our homes, and our family members to You. Lord, may You accept and bless our consecration. Glorify Yourself and greatly use us that each one of us may be filled with the Holy Spirit, have the power of the Holy Spirit, and have the word to contact others. Lord, we pray that You would open the door of the gospel so that those whom we have contacted can come to believe in You and to receive You. May You answer our prayer. Amen.

CHAPTER FOUR

THE OUTLET FOR THE GOSPEL

Scripture Reading: Luke 5:27-29; Acts 5:42; 10:24

THE STORY OF
THE WIND, THE CLOUD, THE FIRE, AND THE ELECTRUM

Hymns, #212 in the Chinese hymnal may be translated literally as follows:

1 The Holy Spirit as a great wind blows from heaven,
Blowing upon us, a multitude, as at Pentecost,
Softening our hardened heart, reviving our whole being,
Blowing until we are renewed and all sins fall away.

Blowing! Blowing! The Holy Spirit, the great wind, blowing!
Covering! Covering! The Spirit, the great cloud, covering!
Burning! Burning! The holy fire burning!
Glowing! Glowing! God's electrum glowing!

2 The Spirit as a great cloud comes with God's abundant
grace,
Covering all of us, as covering the Tent of Meeting,
That we may have life and be sanctified,
Making us spiritual to be God's dwelling.

3 The holy consuming fire comes to burn me,
Reaching every corner to purify me,
Burning away all that is defiled and common,
That I may be exactly like God, holy and without blemish.

4 The glowing electrum shines into me
That I may partake of the divine nature—
God's nature mingled with man's, man's spirit joined
to God's—
That God's life may be expressed in human form.

Twenty-three years ago when I was giving the Life-study of Ezekiel in Taipei, I wrote this hymn concerning the wind, the cloud, the fire, and the electrum based on the vision revealed in Ezekiel 1. Strictly speaking, wind is not good, a cloud is not very welcome, and fire is even worse. In Ezekiel 1, however, the wind, the cloud, and the fire all signify the Holy Spirit.

The coming of wind and a cloud indicates the outbreak of war and troubles. Once the Holy Spirit comes, there is also trouble. The Holy Spirit comes first as a storm wind and then as a great cloud, bringing war. This war first starts within you, causing you to war against yourself. The believers in the Lord all had this experience at the time they heard the gospel. When you hear the gospel and the Holy Spirit starts to work, your inner being is in turmoil as you struggle whether or not to receive the gospel. This is the wind with the cloud stirring in you. Simultaneously, a great fire is kindled to burn away all the negative things in you. Eventually, the electrum is produced.

Electrum is an alloy of silver and gold. Gold, signifying the nature of God, is the base of the New Jerusalem. Without gold as the base, the city cannot be built. The Christian life is a life based upon the golden nature of God. If we do not have God as our golden base, our Christian life is a mess, and we are not able to be built up as part of God's building.

What this hymn describes is the work of the Holy Spirit. The first stanza says that the Holy Spirit as a storm wind blows not from the four corners of the earth but from heaven, that is, from God. When this wind blows upon us, we hear the gospel, and there is a strong stirring within us. The blowing eventually softens our hardened heart and enlivens our entire being so that we are completely renewed and altogether freed from our sins. In Genesis chapter one, at the beginning of God's creation, His Spirit brooded like a hen over her chicks. Similarly, stanza 2 says that when the great wind covers and overshadows us, it broods over us to regenerate us, sanctify us, and make us spiritual that we may be the dwelling place of God.

Stanza 3 says that the Holy Spirit as the fire comes also to burn within us. Once we believe in the Lord, our first experience is a battle, a warring within. We were once wicked, filthy, and fond of worldly entertainment. But now that we have believed in the Lord, the Holy Spirit begins to rule within us, and there is conflict. From the time the conflict starts, the fire comes forth, spreading intensely to every corner to consume all the things that displease God. The fire burns away all defilements and all common things, thereby purifying us so that we may be exactly like God, holy and without blemish. Stanza 4 says that the glowing electrum is manifested and shines into our heart that we may partake of God's nature. The result is that divinity is mingled with humanity, and the human spirit is joined to the divine Spirit; thus, God's life is expressed through us.

This is the story of Ezekiel chapter one. When the Holy Spirit blows, He is like a great wind and a cloud coming to brood and to hatch. He is also like the burning fire which burns away everything other than God; this burning produces God. Ultimately, what comes out of the wind, the cloud, the fire, and the electrum is a person—the Lord Jesus sitting on the throne as the One who expresses God in His humanity, as seen by Ezekiel in 1:26. The four Gospels in the New Testament describe the Lord Jesus from four angles. The Gospel of Luke shows us that the Lord Jesus was a man in whose human virtues the divine attributes were expressed. That was divinity mingled with humanity and the human spirit joined to the divine Spirit so that God's life could be expressed in the form of man, which is divinity expressed through humanity.

THE POWER OF THE GOSPEL

To many in the Pentecostal movement, the power of the gospel is related mostly to speaking in tongues, divine healing, and casting out demons. However, the Bible does not say this. In 1932 I began to pay attention to the matter of speaking in tongues. Then in 1936 I personally attended Pentecostal meetings for over a year and spoke in tongues with them. Afterward I felt I had no taste for this, and I did not know what to think about it. I went back to the Bible and spent more time to study this matter of speaking in tongues. I discovered that the Bible does not say that speaking in tongues, divine healing, and the casting out of demons are the power of the gospel. The book of Acts specifically shows us that when the apostles preached the gospel, they drew their power from the Spirit of God and the word of God through their prayer and speaking of God's word. I have studied this book for many years, and it is more and more clear to me that the power of the gospel lies in two items—God's Spirit and God's word—and it also lies in two matters—prayer and the speaking of God's word.

The book of Acts mentions three times that the word of God "grew" (6:7; 12:24; 19:20). The Bible reveals that God's word is the seed of life (1 Pet. 1:23-25). Because this seed is living, once it is planted it grows, increases, and spreads.

Essentially speaking, the power of the gospel is God's Spirit and God's word. On our side, however, we need to do something to cooperate. Today God's Spirit is upon us and God's word is within us. What we should do is pray that God's Spirit will be our power. God's Spirit is like the air, and our prayer is our spiritual breathing. The air is here, but if we do not breathe, we do not receive the sustenance. God's Spirit is here, but we still need to breathe by prayer. Acts 1 says that the Holy Spirit would come upon the disciples, but they had to pray first. To this end, one hundred twenty saints prayed in one accord for ten days, and the Holy Spirit was poured out. The Holy Spirit has been ultimately consummated, but prayer is still needed to receive the Holy Spirit.

As for God's word, in Acts 6:4 Peter said, "But we will continue steadfastly in prayer and in the ministry of the word." This indicates that the word of God needs to be preached. On the one hand, if we do not properly read the word of God, we cannot preach it. On the other hand, if we do not preach the word of God, we cannot properly read it. We may illustrate this with teaching. On the one hand, a person cannot be a teacher unless he is first a student. On the other hand, those who are teachers know that regardless of how well they study from books, mere studying cannot be compared to teaching, because the need to teach forces them to read thoroughly. Therefore, in order to preach, one must read, and when one reads, he must preach.

In Greek, to *continue steadfastly* implies to continue without ceasing. When we pray, we pray with the Spirit; when we preach, we preach the word. Whether praying or preaching, we need to do it continually. The Spirit is already here, but if we do not pray, He will not move; once we pray, He moves. Prayer is to move the Spirit. The Pentecostals seem to say that only by speaking in tongues, receiving spiritual baptism, and rolling on the floor or jumping can a person receive the Spirit. Do not listen to their wrong teachings. I did some of those things, and after being in the Lord's work for more than fifty years, I can testify that what they claim is altogether not true.

THE STORY OF THE HOLY SPIRIT

Our Triune God today has passed through all the processes and has completed everything that needed to be done. He completed creation, and He also passed through incarnation, human living, crucifixion, and resurrection to become the consummated life-giving Spirit. He is the essential Spirit and also the economical Spirit. He is within us as the Spirit of life, and He is also outside of us as the Spirit of power. This all-inclusive, immeasurable Spirit is our Triune God. Much of Christianity believes that the Father is on the throne, the Son is sitting at His right hand, and only the Holy Spirit comes to us. Even though doctrinally it seems this way, actually in our experience the Father, the Son, and the Spirit are the one Spirit. He is our Redeemer and our Savior; He is the consummated, all-inclusive Spirit. He is right here, and He is within us.

You young people are so blessed to get to know these truths. Today the Triune God is the all-inclusive Spirit dwelling in you. You can pray to Him and contact Him. He is the wonderful Spirit. The more you read His Word, consider His works, and preach His word, the more you will believe into Him. It is by praying sincerely that you can contact the wonderful Triune God who dwells in you. Once you pray, the wind will blow upon you. Then when the wind comes, it becomes the cloud to brood over you like a brooding hen, hatching its chicks. Once the cloud broods over you, you will have the burning within. You may often think of yourself as very clever and rational, but once the fire starts to burn, you will be fervent and become "crazy."

The burning of the fire will purify you from sins, causing you to confess, to admit, that you are truly corrupt because you do things such as talk back to your parents, throw your chopsticks in anger, and lose your temper. Once you confess, more and more exposure will come. We may use cleaning your house as an illustration. You may think that the house is clean, but once you start cleaning, you discover dust everywhere, and it seems impossible to completely clean it. Maybe you do not sin, but since you live in a world that is filled with evil and filth, you cannot help but be defiled. Regardless of how often you have washed your hands, when you wipe them with a handkerchief, the handkerchief is dirty. You did not touch any coal, but when you wipe your hand with the handkerchief a few times, it becomes black. Therefore, do not think that you have no sin. In fact, your sins are as many as the grains of sand on the seashore. One time I confessed in this way; the more I confessed, the more confession I had to make. I confessed that everyone I contacted was offended by me, and everything I did was wrong. That confession took one hour.

Nevertheless, while you are confessing, you are breathing in the Spirit. This Spirit comes to you both as the essential Spirit and the economical Spirit. He fills you inwardly and is upon you to be your power. You can receive power without having to speak in tongues. This power comes from the wind, the cloud, and the fire. The wind, the cloud, and the fire come from your prayer and your enjoyment. In every meeting we have to pray with our spirit and enjoy the Lord. This will produce the wind, the cloud, and the fire. The more we are exercised in our spirit, the more we will ignite the fire. The result will be that both our college campuses and our neighbors will be stirred up by us.

Forty years ago, I often led the church to preach the gospel in Chefoo. Many times when we preached, there was an "ocean of fire"; the ball of fire burned everywhere. It burned to a point that the outsiders said to one another, "You had better not go to the upper floor where they meet. Once you go up there, you will not be able to withstand the fire. It will surely engulf you." There was a power, a ball of strong fire, that was burning. This burning came from the Holy Spirit. The Spirit is already here, but we need to ignite Him by our enjoyment and prayer. Therefore, instead of listening to the wrong teachings of Christianity, we should come back to the Bible. The Bible shows us that the Spirit has already come; on the night of the Lord's resurrection He was breathed into the disciples, and on the day of Pentecost He came upon them. Therefore, there is no need for us to beg for the Spirit to come today. Rather, we should pray that the Spirit would burn within us, causing us to deal with all of our sins that He may move and operate within us.

A certain co-worker once testified that I do not have eloquence, but if you listen to my preaching, you will be subdued. It is true that I do not have eloquence, but you cannot withstand my speaking. I simply speak, and you give in. My secret is this: Every time before I release a message, if I do not pray first, I feel incapable and powerless, but once I pray, the fire is ignited in only ten minutes. As soon as the fire starts to burn within me, I become crazy, and I have to burn you too. Therefore, the power of the gospel is the moving of the Spirit. For the Spirit to move, we need to pray and have enjoyment. If we do not pray, the Spirit will have no way to move.

SPEAKING GOD'S WORD

God's word is also the power of the gospel. God's word needs us to speak it forth. However, if we have not learned to properly study the word of God, we will have no way to speak it. Fifty-five years ago I was called by the Lord. I had the burden to minister the word for the Lord. However, as soon as I opened my mouth, I felt my lack of words. I could speak no more than two sentences. I could only say that it is wonderful to believe in Jesus; I did not know what else to say. This forced me to diligently read through the Bible. I read more and more, and as a result I have a more thorough understanding of the word, and I also have more to speak.

The publications in the Lord's recovery today are not poor as were publications sixty years ago. Moreover, they have already been translated into many different languages. There are enough messages for you to read for many years. Therefore, you cannot make the excuse that you do not understand or do not know how to speak. If you want to understand, you need to go read. Once you read, you have to speak; and the more you speak, the clearer it will be. Every time I have released a message, it has been the case that the more I spoke, the clearer it got. It is the same with writing the footnotes of the Recovery Version; the more I write, the more light I receive. As spirit and life, the Lord's word is power. The Bible says that no word from God shall be void of power (Luke 1:37 ASV), and those who hear the word of the Lord will live (John 5:25). When you preach the gospel, you have to preach the Lord's word. You cannot merely tell people that it is wonderful to believe in Jesus and that our church is very good. The more you say that, the less interested they will be. You have to give the Lord's word to them to convince them. Therefore, you have to learn to speak the Lord's word.

The Lord has truly given us great mercy by unveiling His word completely to us and allowing us to publish what we have seen so that we can study it. Therefore, today the Spirit is here, and the word is also here. We need to pray with the Spirit, and we also need to preach the word. If we continue to pray with the Spirit and preach the word, we will become "crazy." Reading books on philosophy can never cause us to be crazy; but as soon as we read God's word, we will become crazy from within. I have read the writings of Confucius, and I did not become crazy. While reading the Lord's word, however, I often have become abundantly excited with an indescribable joy. This is because there is no spirit in Confucius's books, but there is spirit in the Lord's word. The Lord said that the words which He has spoken to us are spirit and are life (John 6:63). If we do not read the Lord's word, His word will be stationary, not "moving" or "jumping." However, as soon as we read the Lord's word, it will start to move within us, causing us to start moving as well.

There was a co-worker among us named Luan Hong-bin,

who was from Manchuria. Formerly he was involved in politics and therefore greatly despised and opposed Christianity. He thought that only those Chinese who could not support themselves would turn to a Western religion for help and that any Chinese with integrity would not believe it. One day while he was on a hill, he entered into a temple and saw an open Bible on the table of sacrifice. Even though he did not like Christianity, he was still curious to find out what the Bible says. He looked, and it was open to Psalm 1: "Blessed is the man / Who does not walk / In the counsel of the wicked, / Nor stand on the path of sinners, / Nor sit in the seat of mockers" (v. 1). He thought this was interesting, so he read on. Eventually, he was captured by the Lord's word. He rolled on the floor, cried in confession, repented, and was saved. Later on, he became a good co-worker and changed his name to Philip Luan. One time when I was in Brother Nee's training in Shanghai, I stayed in the same room with him, and he told me this story in person.

There is another story that I can never forget. There was once an American who went to Africa on business. He saw a local African sitting beneath a tree reading the Bible. This American man thought of himself as one who was modern and understood science, so he despised religion and considered it superstition. He said to the man in a disdaining tone, "Do you still read the Bible?" The man answered and said, "Sir, if I had not been reading the Bible and if the words of the Bible had not entered into me, I would have eaten you, and you would right now be in my stomach." This illustrates the power of the Bible.

I studied the matter of speaking in tongues fifty years ago, and I also joined that kind of activity for more than a year. Later, I did not speak in tongues anymore, and I advised others not to practice this. After a few years, when I was in my hometown, Chefoo, not far from the meeting hall there was a Pentecostal church. The responsible brother there had a good relationship with me. One day that brother came to visit me. He wanted me to speak in tongues again, to be in the same flow with him. I asked him to sit down, and with a very serious tone, I said to him, "Brother, I do not speak in tongues now, and I will not take that way of practice. Today I will speak to you openly. Is your preaching more powerful, or is mine? We have been working here for many years. Who is making the greater profit? Is it you or I? The more you preach, the fewer people you have there. The more I preach, the more people we have here. Where is your power?" He said, "Brother Lee, if you put it this way, I have nothing to say. I admit I have not been as successful you. Yet I have to speak in tongues because if I do not speak in tongues, I have no power." I then said, "If this is the case, then go and speak in tongues. The more you speak, the less powerful you will be. However, I will not speak in tongues, and the more I will not speak, the more powerful I will become."

I spoke such words not only to this person but also to others. Later on I also spoke the same words in Taiwan and in America. Sometimes I would say, "You speak in tongues, but where is the fruit of your work? Where is the effectiveness of your work? I dare not say that I have much fruit for my work, but my fruit is at least more than yours. Therefore, speaking in tongues does not work. I do not speak a single phrase of tongues, but I have gained a great number of people." At the end, many who spoke in tongues all had to concede defeat. The secret of my work is not in speaking in tongues but in praying with the Spirit and preaching the word.

CALLING ON THE NAME OF THE LORD

In Taiwan I tried to teach the saints to stir up their spirit, but I was not clear about how to do it. Later when I came to America, I saw clearly that to stir up the spirit is to call on the name of the Lord. In Acts 2 Peter said that when the Holy Spirit is outpoured, everyone who calls on the name of the Lord shall be saved (v. 21). Normally we understand salvation in a shallow way. However, when people asked Peter what they should do, Peter said, "Repent and each one of you be baptized upon the name of Jesus Christ for the forgiveness of your sins, and you will receive the gift of the Holy Spirit" (v. 38). This indicates that the blessing of salvation begins with the forgiveness of sins and consummates with the receiving of the gift of the Holy Spirit. Forgiveness is the initiation, and receiving the Holy Spirit is the consummation. The consummation of our salvation is to receive the Holy Spirit. If we have not received the Spirit, our salvation is not complete. Once we are saved today, we receive the Spirit. However, we need to fan our spirit into flame (2 Tim. 1:6-7). The way to fan our spirit into flame is to pray, to call on the name of the Lord.

It is strange that although we have already received the Spirit, if we do not avail ourselves of the Spirit, everything we do will be to no avail. Without the Spirit, our prophesying will be of no avail. Likewise, without the Spirit, our gospel preaching will be of no avail. In order to have the Spirit, we have to pray, and in our prayer we have to call on the name of the Lord. There is no need to be very proper when we pray; rather, we should be crazy. Fifty years ago, I was taught to be proper when I prayed. I was taught to be sincere when I knelt down, then to pray by the Spirit in the name of the Son to the Holy Father, asking for His grace and blessing. Later on I realized that this is dead prayer. In His prayer and preaching, the Lord Jesus did not keep any regulation or formality. When He preached, He had no podium or time schedule, and there was no program to His speaking. However, there was the power. We also should pray like this, not paying any attention to regulations but rather calling on the name of the Lord unceasingly.

In 1968 we began in America to exercise calling on the name of the Lord. In one meeting I said to the saints, "In your daily life try to forget everything and just call on the Lord's name for ten minutes. Forget about your status and your work; just call on the Lord's name. If you do not become burning, come and see me." I still have the assurance today that if you call on the name of the Lord for only ten minutes, you will be burning. Young people who are on the campuses, if you are burned like this every morning, you will burn others when you are at school. Once the gospel is spoken or preached, there will be the Spirit.

Once when I was in elementary school, the teacher wanted us all to give a speech. I was so frightened that I was shaking and perspiring and did not know what I would say on the platform. Later when I was saved and called by the Lord, I was clear that one day I would have to minister and speak for Him. Therefore, I tried to think of ways to prepare myself. At that time I worked by the sea, and there was a mountain nearby. Behind the mountain it was very quiet. Every day, during my lunch break at noon, I would go to the back of the mountain to practice speaking to the sea. The result was that the more I practiced speaking, the better I became. However, one day a denominational group invited me to speak on the Lord's Day. That was my first time to speak on the podium, so I prepared much at home before going. I spoke on "Behold, the Lamb of God!" At that time, facing more than three hundred people, I was very frightened. Moreover, as no one had ever taught me to use my spirit, when I spoke I did not use my spirit, so my speaking was to no avail. Later I became clear that in order to exercise the spirit, there is the need of praying, calling on the name of the Lord, and reading the Word. These are the sources of the power of the gospel.

THE OUTLET FOR THE GOSPEL

Now we want to see what the mouthpiece and the outlet for the gospel are. The mouthpiece for the gospel is man. Moreover, the outlet for the gospel is the homes. We are the mouthpieces for the gospel, and our homes are the outlets for the gospel. If your home is not given for the Lord's use, and you preach the gospel only individually, then there will be a mouthpiece but no outlet. Acts shows us that at the time of Peter, the disciples not only broke bread "from house to house" (2:46) but also announced Jesus Christ as the gospel "from house to house" (5:42). In Greek, the word *announce* is the verb form of the word *gospel,* meaning that they announced the gospel of Jesus as the Christ. If we announce the gospel of Jesus as the Christ from house to house, then all our houses will be speaking Christ. Hence, we should not only preach the gospel but also open our homes.

Luke 5 gives us an excellent example. The Lord Jesus saw a tax collector named Levi, who was a slave to money, and He called him to follow Him. Upon hearing the Lord's calling, Levi left all, rose up, and followed the Lord. In this way he was saved. Once he was saved, he gave a great reception for the Lord Jesus in his house. However, he did not invite Jesus alone, nor did he invite prominent officials and famous persons. Instead, he invited many tax collectors and sinners (vv. 27-29). Because he himself was a vile sinner, he did not have good men as his friends but rather a crowd of wicked men, all of whom he invited to recline at table with the Lord. The Lord was the guest of honor, and all the other guests invited to keep Him company were sinners. This is a good example of opening the homes for the preaching of the gospel. Once we open our homes, the gospel will have an outlet; without the homes, the gospel will have no outlet. Now we have many mouthpieces, but what we need is the outlet. Hence, we must open our homes.

I hope that all the saints, especially those who are newly saved, will do this one thing—hold a reception for Jesus and invite all of your friends, even the friends who are disreputable. You and I do not have reputable friends. What we have are "sinner-friends," such as drinking friends, gambling friends, dancing friends, playing friends, and deceiving friends. Seriously speaking, where can you find good people on this earth? All are sinners. We did not have good friends before we were saved, but after we got saved, the Lord Jesus became our good Friend. We should hold receptions at our homes for the Lord Jesus and invite our sinner-friends that they may receive the Lord Jesus as their Friend.

The Bible not only has examples of sinners preaching the gospel; it also has examples of "good men" preaching the gospel. In Acts 10 there was a good man, Cornelius. The Bible does not mention any sin of his; it speaks of only his good points. He was a devout man who feared God, gave alms to the people, and always prayed and petitioned before God. One day an angel came to him and said, "Your prayers and your alms have ascended as a memorial before God. And now send...for a certain Simon, who is surnamed Peter" (vv. 4-5). It is true that Cornelius was truly a good man, but he was not saved and still needed the gospel. Therefore, he needed to ask Simon Peter to come and tell him how to be saved. When Peter came, he was surprised because Cornelius was already waiting there, having called together his "relatives and intimate friends" (v. 24). *Relatives and intimate friends* is a very good expression and a good example to us.

The house of Levi, a tax collector, and the house of Cornelius are excellent examples to us. Regardless of whether we are slaves of money, like the tax collectors who were vile sinners, or we are those who often pray to God and give alms to the poor, like Cornelius, who was a virtuous person, we are all sinners before the Lord; we all need salvation. We also need to open our house and hold a reception for Jesus, inviting all our relatives and intimate friends. I believe in that day when the Lord Jesus was with the group of tax collectors, there must have been many who eventually were saved. Perhaps even all of them were saved. I also believe that those relatives and intimate friends who were at the house of Cornelius that day were also saved, with no one left out. Therefore, the way to contact people with the gospel is in the homes. If there are no homes, the gospel will not have a way. When there is a home, the gospel has a way.

The Lord as a great wind blew upon us and brought us to America. The elderly saints never thought about coming to America. When I was in mainland China, I felt it was very good to be there, especially in the three "norths"—North China, the northwest, and the northeast. We could go anywhere in those regions to work for the Lord, so why should we go to a foreign country and stay in a foreign land? In 1938 someone gave me two checks. One was 1,600 U. S. dollars for my fare to America; the other was 1,200 Chinese yuan for my family's living expenses for one year. However, I did not have the burden and never even thought about coming to America. China is so vast and has many people. It would not have been possible for us to cover all the places or to exhaust our preaching of the gospel, so why would we think of coming to America? However, this was not up to us. Eventually the Lord blew upon me, and I was brought to Taiwan and then to America.

Whether or not it was your desire, the Lord blew upon you also and brought you to America. Today the Lord is like a great wind that has blown multitudes of Chinese to America. This is the Lord's perfect will. If men do not leave their own land or soil, they will not believe in the Lord. However, since they have been uprooted and have come to a foreign country, it is easy for them to believe in the Lord. This is why on the college campuses it is easy for us to preach the gospel to the Chinese students. There are hardly any rejections; many have come to attend the Lord's banquet, and nearly all of them have received the Lord. This is the Lord's work.

The Lord saved Levi, a tax collector. This was Matthew, who later became one of the twelve disciples to preach the gospel to many sinners. In the vision that Cornelius saw, the angel did not tell him to invite his relatives and intimate friends. However, he did not hide what he had for only his family members to be brought to salvation. Rather, he invited all of his relatives and intimate friends. We need to take him as our model. When you young people go to the college campuses, you are there to hold a reception for Jesus. Just set out a few cold treats, and use half an hour to share the gospel with the friends. That is your home. Alternately, if you can get your parents' permission, you can invite classmates over for meals and to hear the gospel. The gospel presented in this way will save young people from becoming vile persons, like the American hippies. In America it is dangerous for the young people to not believe in the Lord Jesus. If they do not believe, it is hard to know what they will do because there are all kinds of strange and bizarre things happening on college campuses. Only Jesus can replace those things. If parents are wise, they will definitely let their sons and daughters believe in Jesus.

Therefore, I hope that all of you will open your homes to give a great reception for Jesus, simply inviting "sinners" as your guests that you may preach the gospel to them. If you open your homes, it will not be a loss but a blessing to you. The Lord Himself said that He will show lovingkindness to thousands of generations of those who love Him (Exo. 20:6). Hence, for the sake of eternity, we all should open our homes and provide an outlet for the gospel of the Lord. In this way, the blessing will come not only to us but also to our sons and daughters for generation after generation.

CHAPTER FIVE

HOW TO VISIT PEOPLE BY DOOR-KNOCKING

Scripture Reading: Matt. 28:19; Acts 4:31; Rom. 10:13; Mark 16:16a

THE CARRYING OUT OF THE GOD-ORDAINED WAY FOR INCREASE AND SPREAD

Starting from October of 1984, the Lord has led us anew to have a change in Taipei. This does not mean that the truth among us has changed; the truth will never change. This change is rather a renewing of our way of serving, functioning, and meeting. From many perspectives we studied and observed the church history of the twentieth century to see how the saints on this earth in the churches have served, functioned, and met. We did this to find the proper way that is according to the Lord's leading in the present age with regard to the meetings and service.

The Low Rate of Increase in Christianity

We have spent much time and energy to bring in such a change because we saw that even though the truth in the Lord's recovery is rich, bright, and high, the increase in the number of saints among us has been very slow and low. We have studied the rates of increase of all the Christian groups as well as other major religious groups in human society, observing how they propagate. This is not to say that we intend to imitate them. Rather, we did this for comparison and reference. The thing that made us feel most ashamed is that among the five major religions, the one that has had the highest rate of propagation in the last few centuries is Islam. Their increase is measured not by percentage but rather by multiples. The rate of increase of Christians, however, has been extremely low.

I came to start the work in the United States in 1962. In the summer of 1964, a brother who was a worker in the Southern Baptist denomination showed us their statistics. The report indicated that in 1964 the Southern Baptist denomination had eleven million members. In 1985 their number increased by another three million, bringing the total to fourteen million. From the numerical point of view, this is very impressive. However, considering that this took place within twenty-two years, the rate of increase is only about 1.5 percent, not even 2 percent. This shows that their rate of increase is very low, and the spread is very slow. The rate of increase and spread of Christianity's largest group—the Catholic Church—is also very low. Because of this, we felt even more that there is the need to study the situation.

The Cases of the Mormons and the Jehovah's Witnesses

The strange thing is that the two great heretical groups within Christianity, the Mormons and the Jehovah's Witnesses, have had the fastest increase and spread within the past one hundred years. We have examined the publications of Mormonism and have found their literature heretical. They say that Jesus Christ was born of Mary and Adam. What other heresy can be greater than this? They acknowledge Jesus Christ, they also refer to the Bible, and they speak about the Holy Spirit. They explain the former rain and the latter rain in the Old Testament book of Joel by saying that the Holy Spirit descending on the day of Pentecost is the former rain, while the Holy Spirit descending in the future is the latter rain. Therefore, they call themselves the "Church of Jesus Christ of Latter-day Saints." However, they say in blasphemy that the one in whom they believe and whom they preach was born of Mary and Adam.

Recently when I went to the mountains to rest, I contacted a real-estate agent there who was an upright man and also a member of the Jehovah's Witnesses. One day he came to my resting place for a special visit. During the course of our conversation I found out that he is a zealous person who always sets aside two days out of the week for the purpose of door-knocking. When we came to some theological issues, I asked him, "Who is this Jesus Christ whom you worship and serve? Is He God?" He answered, "Jesus Christ is not the eternal God, who has no beginning and no ending. Since Jesus Christ has a beginning, He is not the eternal God, but the archangel Michael." Right away, I opened up Romans 9:5 to show him that Jesus Christ "is God over all, blessed forever." After he read it, he said that the punctuation marks in this verse are wrong. I said, "That is your way of taking it out of context. This verse in Greek clearly indicates that Jesus Christ is God, who is over all and blessed forever." I say this to let you see that these two groups are heretical, but they are the fastest growing groups among all the groups in Christianity. They have the highest rate of increase of members. Therefore, we have to ask ourselves why it seems that we cannot spread out even though the truth is rich, the light is clear, and the vision is high among us in the Lord's recovery?

Testimonies of the Expansion of the Lord's Recovery in Taiwan

When I started laboring in Taiwan in 1949, I made a decision that we should propagate the gospel in an aggressive way. What we did in Taipei is an example. We divided each district according to different streets and lanes. The brothers and sisters would claim a portion until each street and lane were claimed. The saints went from house to house to pass out gospel tracts until they covered all of Taipei. At the same time, we posted gospel banners such as "God loves the world" and "Christ Jesus came into the world to save sinners" on the big streets, small lanes, intersections, bus stops, and the doors of the houses of the brothers and sisters. There was also a gospel team that went out to proclaim the gospel in the evenings in the middle of the week. On the Lord's Day, different teams took their route into the New Park. Every Lord's Day afternoon, the three thousand seats at the amphitheater in the New Park were filled. We were able to bring back four hundred gospel name cards. The next night we distributed the cards to the brothers and sisters so that they could right away go door-knocking and visiting. Because of this, a great number of people were saved. Not only did we do this in Taipei, but other localities also practiced this. Therefore, when the work began in Taiwan, there were only three to five hundred people, but in five or six years the number increased one hundredfold, reaching forty to fifty thousand people. From this we also learned a lesson, realizing that we cannot only pray without taking any action. Prayer is first, but following the prayer there should be action. Only in this way can the Lord bless us.

In 1957 when we invited Brother T. Austin-Sparks to come and visit us, a small distraction ensued, causing the one accord among us to be damaged. From that time on, the increase of the Lord's recovery has been going downhill. When I left the country and stayed overseas for more than twenty years, the number almost did not increase at all because there was the lack of proper action. We studied this segment of our history, and after making comparisons we felt that we needed to restore a proper action. In Matthew 28:18 and 19, the Lord Jesus said, "All authority has been given to Me in heaven and on earth. Go therefore." The Lord already has the authority, but if we do not go, it is impossible to have the increase. This shows us that on the Lord's side He has the authority, the power, but on our side we need to cooperate, to take action.

Starting from October of 1984, we studied this matter in Taipei, and we started to experiment. I also told the brothers and sisters that from that day on, all of our meetings, services, and activities would have to be changed thoroughly. We needed to put aside what we had from the past. We thank and praise the Lord that up to the first half of this year, our experiment has proved to be correct and totally practical. In this message I first want to fellowship a result that came out of our experiment: We should go door-knocking and preach the gospel from house to house in the communities and on the college campuses, not to people we are familiar with but by knocking on "strange" doors. Due to the influence of our backgrounds and past experiences, we have always felt that we would be turned down if we knock on a stranger's door. However, our experiment has proved that as long as we are willing to knock, the door will open. Therefore, with this kind of situation, we have to learn how to visit by door-knocking.

THE PREREQUISITE FOR VISITING PEOPLE BY DOOR-KNOCKING—THE PERSON HIMSELF

It is true that in cooperating with prayer, we should take action and go out to visit by door-knocking. However, your person is crucial when it comes to door-knocking. Due to our persons, your visiting may be one way, and my visiting may be another way; if the president were to visit people, he would do it in yet another way. Therefore, there have to be some requirements for visitation by door-knocking. First, you must be one who loves and seeks the Lord. Second, you must be one who pursues the truth and is learned in truth. Third, you must be one who grows in life and is being transformed day by day. Fourth, you must be one who deals often with sins, prays before the Lord, and is always filled by the Holy Spirit. Fifth, you must be one who has had a change in character because of the life that is within you. In order to go out visiting people by door-knocking, you need to be equipped with these fundamental requirements.

Using a colloquial expression, we may describe the shortcoming of the Chinese as being loose and sloppy. In the spring of this year, there were over one hundred college graduates who joined the Full-time Training in Taipei. I have had two classes with them every week. Once I said to them, "Your hair is not properly combed; it looks so messy. Will people listen to you when you go and preach the gospel to them? Look at yourselves. Your ties do not match in color, your shirts are not coordinated, your socks look even worse, and who knows how long it has been since you last polished your shoes. If this is the way you look, when you stand there giving a message or sit there to preach the gospel to others, who will listen to you? A Chinese proverb says, 'Words from a man of lowly position carry little weight.' This means that if you are a light person, your speaking will be light as well. When people see that you do not look like a proper person yet you are trying to preach the gospel to them to get them saved, they may think that you should be saved first before you come and get them saved." Thank and praise the Lord that after I said that, the next time I went to the class I saw that the brothers had combed their hair neatly and the sisters had changed their clothes. They all dressed properly and suitably, and their shoes were brightly polished.

If you truly love the Lord, desire the truth, pursue the growth in life, frequently confess your sins, receive dealings before the Lord, and are being filled with the Holy Spirit, you will be improved in your character. If you have a good character when you go out to visit people, they will give you a certain amount of respect from the moment they open the door. But when you go to knock on doors, if your hair is messy, your tie is crooked and does not match your clothes, and your shoes are not polished, then people may open the door to let you in, and they may ask you to sit down, but the more they observe you, the more they will feel that you are not proper. After being examined by them for a few minutes, you will be too embarrassed to speak, and you will lose your standing. Therefore, for us to propagate and for the number of people to increase, we need to be thoroughly changed and equipped anew.

THE LAW OF EFFECTIVE DOOR-KNOCKING

Praying, Confessing Our Sins, Dealing with Our Sins, and Being Filled with the Holy Spirit

When we go door-knocking in the community and on the campuses, we must know how to do it. First of all, every time before we go out, we must have adequate and thorough prayer until we are filled with the Holy Spirit. Once we turn to our spirit and pray to the Lord, our inner being will be enlightened. We will sense many things that are improper, as though we have come to a mirror and seen our real situation. At that time, we have to confess our sins, the more the better. This will cause us to deal with our sins. When we have nothing more to confess is when the Holy Spirit fills us. When all of our trespasses and sins have been emptied out, the Holy

Spirit will fill our entire being. Then we will have the boldness to go door-knocking.

Being filled with the Holy Spirit is like breathing. Breathing is a continual matter. If we hold our breath for three minutes, we will die. Hence, every time we go to visit people, we first have to pray earnestly. Even though we prayed yesterday, we have to pray again for our going out today and come before the Lord for His shining. In our daily walk in the world we are always being defiled; thus, we need to be cleansed again and again. This may be likened to washing our hands. Although I do not usually do the cleaning at home and try my best not to touch anything dirty, I still have to wash my hands seven to eight times a day. In the same way, no matter how thoroughly you prayed and confessed to the Lord yesterday, you still have to pray thoroughly today before you go out to visit people and bring the Lord to them. You cannot omit this time of prayer. You must pay the price for this. If you are serious in this matter, you will realize that it is not enough to spend merely three to five minutes to pray.

It is an unalterable law that to pray until we are filled with the Holy Spirit requires us to be enlightened and to confess our sins. The more silent we are before the Lord and the more we are open to Him, the more sense we will have within. That sense is the Lord's speaking to us; it is the Lord's shining. The Lord speaks to us by the sense we have. As this sense becomes clearer and clearer and the Lord's shining becomes brighter and brighter, we will see our mistakes. We need to confess our sins one by one and deal with them as we sense the Lord's shining. The Lord may shine on you to show you that your anger at your wife this morning was not right. After confessing this to the Lord, He may say, "Now that you have confessed your sin to Me, you need to go to your wife to apologize." This puts you in a difficult position. If you stop here and do not go and apologize, you will be finished. In this condition you will not be effective in your door-knocking. Amazingly, if you do go and apologize and come again before the Lord, you will immediately be filled with the Holy Spirit. You will feel the "wind" of the Spirit passing through you. Then your going out to knock on doors will go well.

This is not a coincidence; rather, this is a spiritual law. If you have some knots within you that you cannot be freed from, how are you going to free others? If you yourself are not saved, how are you going save others? In other words, we need to let the Lord first save us to the uttermost until we are freed; then when we go out door-knocking, we can save others. We might be able to pretend in other matters, but we cannot pretend in this matter. One can tell by looking at the fruit. I hope that we will seriously be exercised in this matter before the Lord.

To pray, to confess our sins, to deal with our sins, and subsequently to be filled with the Holy Spirit will result in boldness and confidence. If you go out door-knocking but have not prayed, your legs will be shaking, and you will not have power in your speaking. However, through prayer, confessing of sins, and being filled with the Holy Spirit, not only will you have the boldness when door-knocking, but you will also have the confidence that the person you are visiting will be saved. If you have not been filled with the Holy Spirit, you might not be able to speak even a word out of your mouth. Once you are filled with the Holy Spirit though, not only will you have the power for speaking, but you also can determine whether or not he will be saved. If you say he will be saved, he will be saved; if you say he will not be saved and that he needs to wait awhile, then he will not be saved. This is the effectiveness of prayer, confessing of sins, and being filled with the Holy Spirit.

Exercising to Speak Wisely

When you go door-knocking, you have to pay attention to your attitude. You should never be reckless or hasty. Rather, you should be modest, courteous, gentle, respectful, dignified, and weighty. Moreover, when you speak, you should learn to be concise instead of being wordy and to be affectionate instead of being cold. If you are too wordy and mechanical, people may close their door immediately or find an excuse to reject you. Thus, you have to exercise to speak straightforwardly, directly, affectionately, and politely. If they answer, "I do not have time," you should not give up. Instead, you should say, "It will take you just one minute." Eventually, the person may be saved and baptized because of this one-minute gospel preaching. It is because we have had this kind of experience that we practice the "one-minute gospel."

Even if you have learned all the truths, a person whom you visit by knocking on his door will not be able to discern that. However, if you take out a book and open it to read with him, his attitude will instantly become more respectful. This also was one of the results of our experiment in Taipei. Anything that is printed in a volume or published as a book is something that is not common. Words that are trivial will not be printed in a book. It does not matter who the person is or how high his speaking skill is, no one can speak as neatly and concisely as a book. The words used in our books have been considered over and over again during the course of writing. Therefore, the wording and the phrasing are clearer and more concise. One co-worker told me, "I found out that while door-knocking, especially on the college campuses, it is useless to speak our own words. The more efficient way is to read our publications. Sometimes I simply open up the Recovery Version and ask the person to read a paragraph of a footnote, and he gets saved." He also uses the life-studies from time to time. He simply opens them for the person to read a section, and the person gets saved. The words of the footnotes in our Recovery Version are refined and pure, and they are also the crucial truths. Some of the sections in our life-studies are also very important. We need to learn to use these.

The booklet *The Mystery of Human Life* has also been greatly used by the Lord in this year. I believe that the total print quantity of this booklet in all the localities is about one million copies. Hence, we also have to learn to use this booklet. While using it, do not be wordy; furthermore, the shorter the time you take the better. First, you should memorize the four main sections. The first section is on God's creation, the second section is on man's fall, the third section is on Christ's redemption, and the fourth section is on God's dispensing. While you are reading with someone, do not read from the beginning to the end in a dead and rigid way. You need to learn to follow the Spirit's leading within you. When you sense you need to read a certain section, then turn to that section and read it. Do not read too much; if you read too much, you will lose the Lord in the reading. A sales person once told me that the technique to making sales is not to speak too much. Just speak a few sentences that are clear and concise, and then draw the person to say, "Very good." Once you hear this word, you should immediately say, "Very good; please buy one!" and take out your order book. Because he has already said it is good, he will be reluctant to refuse.

Learning to Grasp the Opportunity

A brother once testified that the person he visited said that his speaking was very good. I instructed those present that this was the right moment to "tie the knot" and lead that person to pray. If that person would pray, he would believe and receive the Lord, and then the brother should baptize him. However, if he would not grasp the opportunity but would continue to talk, the opportunity may slip away, and he would not be able to "close the deal." However, some brothers present said, "We are afraid that this is too fast; we are still strangers to one another." Such a consideration means that it is not the new one who is not willing to pray, but it is you who are not willing to pray. It is not that he is not willing to lose his face, but it is you who are not willing to lose your face in leading the prayer. I am speaking these things from my experience. It was the same with me in the past. When I went to lead someone to the Lord, often at the critical juncture I did not have the boldness to lead him to pray. Instead, I kept thinking that it might be too early and that I should not take the opportunity. Once I lost the opportunity, though, I may have lost it for my whole life; I may never have had the opportunity to see him again.

Brother Nee once told us that gospel preachers have to be thick-skinned. Those who are thin-skinned cannot lead people to salvation. Perhaps some brothers and sisters would say, "If this is the case, then since I am such a thin-skinned person, I may as well forget about going out to knock on doors." You may do so as long as you have the peace, but everyone else will still continue to knock on doors. In the past, when I saw strangers, I would start sweating, and my face would turn red.

Every time my mother wanted to invite people to our home, I would be the first one to object because I did not like to meet strangers, and I disliked even more going to other people's homes. Therefore, when I had to preach the gospel to others and lead them to pray at the end, I could not relax my face or open my mouth. Later the Lord arranged the environment and forced me into a situation in which I had to stand and speak from the platform. It does not matter if you are thin-skinned; as long as you are willing to practice, willing to go visit by door-knocking, slowly you will have the boldness. On the other hand, while you are door-knocking, you must learn the technique of grasping the opportunity to lead a person to believe and pray. Immediately after he prays, you should show him Romans 10:13, which says, "For 'whoever calls upon the name of the Lord shall be saved.'" Then say to him, "My friend, congratulations! You are saved!" The next thing is to lead him to be baptized.

Before October of 1984, I did not thoroughly study the Bible regarding the most appropriate way of baptism. Christianity has unceasingly debated the two ways of baptism—baptism by immersion or baptism by sprinkling. Baptism by immersion is to put the entire person into the water, whereas baptism by sprinkling is merely to drop some water on the person. The Bible speaks only about the need for baptism, but it does not emphasize the method of baptism. After one and a half years of door-knocking, our study has shown us that the important matter is not how we baptize people but how to baptize people at the opportune time. Sometimes the person we visit has already believed and received the Lord; he has already prayed to be saved. In this case we must baptize him immediately. If we insist on a method, such as bringing him to the meeting hall's baptistery to be baptized, then before we reach the meeting hall, he probably will have changed his mind and made up excuses to not be baptized. There have been times when some people already had arrived at the meeting hall to be baptized; however, when they were about to change their clothes, they rejected the idea and ran away. Therefore, you have to carry out the baptism while "the iron is still hot." Once you see the opportunity, you should grasp it and baptize people. There are many new and modern apartment buildings in Taipei where there is a big bathtub in the bathroom, and the temperature of the water is easily managed to be hot or cold. As long as there is the opportunity for baptism, the sisters can go fill the tub with water while others are praying. Then after the prayer, the brothers can baptize the person. Sometimes the bathtub is big enough only for the lower part of the body to be baptized. In that case we can pour water on the upper part. This kind of baptism by half immersion and half pouring is also convenient. Hence, do not pay attention to the form but rather to the Spirit.

Exercising to Continue Steadfastly

Beginning from this August, the saints who are coming to join the Full-time Training in Taipei will include almost five hundred from Taiwan, close to one hundred fifty from America, twenty or more from Europe, and a few from South America and Africa. Thus, the number of trainees will be well over six hundred fifty. Including twenty to thirty language class teachers, the total will be over seven hundred. This time the training has one regulation, that is, that the trainees have to go out and visit people two mornings a week and also visit the community and college campuses every afternoon and on the evenings when there are no scheduled meetings. Each of the seven hundred trainees should baptize at least one person per week. In this way, two thousand eight hundred people will be baptized in just a few weeks. I hope that from now on not only the full-time trainees but also each elder and co-worker will practice door-knocking and visiting people. This is the first item we should practice. Maybe we cannot go out to knock on doors every day, but one thing we can do is spend two to three hours each week for door-knocking. We should visit not only those whom we know but also those we do not know. We should knock on all the doors in the district in which we live. Do not worry or be anxious. As long as we are willing to do it, we will be successful.

THE NEW WAY BEING THE GOD-ORDAINED WAY

The result of our study and experiment this year in Taipei

has proven that the new way surely is the God-ordained way. First, we discovered that many high-rise and apartment managers are brothers who have not been meeting with us regularly. When we enter into a high-rise building or an apartment, we have to go through the manager to get his permission. If the manager is not a Christian, once he hears that you have come to preach the gospel, he may have a long face and ask you to leave, not welcoming you or paying attention to you. However, the Lord has confirmed His new way. When many of the managers heard that we were preaching the gospel, they immediately welcomed us and said, "Thank the Lord, I also am a brother. I just have not been coming to the meetings." In this way, not only was the door opened, but he was also invisibly stirred up and recovered.

Second, in the recent twenty to thirty years, there have been a great number of people who were baptized in Taipei. Even though we have used computers to study the statistics, we still cannot determine exactly how many there have been. The number is close to one hundred thousand. Many among them were not meeting with us for a long time, but they were discovered again through the house-to-house visitation. They all welcomed us to come to their homes to start a home meeting. Third, we have also knocked on the doors of many believers who are in the denominations. They also love the Lord and pursue the Lord. Because of their desire for the truth, they were attracted by our practice of the new way, and they turned to the Lord's recovery. Fourth, many unbelievers believed and were baptized. These results are of many aspects, yet they are linked together and closely interrelated. They all have had a great effect on the increase and spread of the Lord's recovery. Therefore, according to the result of the study, we were able to draw a conclusion: The new way is surely the best way ordained by God. There is no better way than this.

We also have become clear that when we go out to knock on doors, we should bring not only the booklet *The Mystery of Human Life* but also some other books, such as the life-studies and the Recovery Version of the New Testament. As to which books to bring with you, you first need to pray. If you walk according to the spirit, you will realize that in your

door-knocking you will often meet someone who is very pur-
suing. At this time, you may ask him to read a section of the
footnotes in the Recovery Version or give him some literature.
In this way, not only do we preach the gospel but we also use
the opportunity to preach and spread the truth. Recently,
some serving ones from the ministry office went out for fellowship and were resting in the mountains. While they were
singing hymns and praying, an old retired woman who lived
across the street heard them and came over to see them. She
was happy to be gathered together with the Lord's believers.
She was also a believer who loved the Lord and was attending
the Southern Baptist denomination. The sisters read to her a
portion of the footnote concerning the five women in Jesus
Christ's genealogy in Matthew 1. After she listened, she said,
"This book is wonderful. Where can I buy it?" The sisters then
gave one to her. She was so happy and immediately said, "I
will prepare a breakfast tomorrow; let us eat together." The
next day after they ate breakfast, right before they were
about to leave she said, "I am the owner of this house. From
now on whenever you want to come to the mountain, please
give me a call. I will welcome your visitation." This proves
that the new way is truly the best way. Not only can it send
out the gospel to save people, turn people back to the Lord, or
search out the backsliding saints, but it also can send out the
truths.

THE BELIEVERS' PREACHING OF THE GOSPEL
BRINGING JOY TO THEMSELVES
AND BLESSINGS TO SOCIETY

I hope that the saints in the Lord's recovery will all accept
the God-ordained new way. Perhaps you have just been newly
saved, or perhaps you have been saved for a long while but
have never been taught in this way. In any case, you all must
admit that the most joyful thing on earth is to lead people to
salvation. Luke 15 tells us that when a sinner repents, there
is joy in heaven (v. 7). The Father also is happy (vv. 23-24, 32).
Seriously speaking, there is no other thing that profits human
society more than the preaching of the gospel. Whether in
America or in Taiwan, the need of the whole society is the

gospel. Because Taiwan has widespread wealth and much indulgence in pleasures, sins have multiplied. It is even more so in America; there is danger everywhere because sinful things abound. How can the Lord bless in this kind of sinful condition? The Christians are the most blessed people because they have received the redemption of the Lord Jesus by faith to enjoy His salvation. Christians are happiest when they preach the gospel to lead people to salvation, which even causes society to be blessed.

COORDINATING WITH THE MOVE OF GOSPELIZING THE WHOLE EARTH

We also hope that in the Lord's recovery there will be one full-timer out of every twenty people. Taipei is practicing this arrangement. There already are one thousand young people who have received this burden. We hope that the number could increase to two thousand five hundred. In this way in just one year, we will be able to gospelize the whole of Taiwan. There are schools and communities everywhere in America, so there is a greater need of full-timers to go out and work for the Lord. However, this move of gospelization is not only the full-timers' responsibility; it is also the responsibility of every saint. Therefore, every saint should set aside at least two to three hours a week to go out to visit people. We will definitely see the fruit after a long period of practice.

On the other hand, in order to produce more full-timers, there is the need for more financial offerings. If indeed there will be two thousand five hundred full-timers in Taiwan, the churches' expenditures will be huge. Hence, we each need to give a portion, putting forth not only our shoulders but also our material possessions. In Luke 16:9 the Lord Jesus said, "And I say to you, Make friends for yourselves by means of the mammon of unrighteousness, so that when it fails, they may receive you into the eternal tabernacles." You may forget what you offered in this age, but this amount is remembered in heaven. Even in eternity, those who have received help through your giving will never forget what you spent on them. They will do their best to repay you. This is the most blessed thing. This is not to say that we should pawn all our belongings or sell all of our possessions in order to have something to offer to the Lord. Rather, we need to give what we can according to what the Lord has given to each of us. Material things will eventually be consumed. Moreover, they can be used only in this age; they will never follow you or be there to welcome you in the eternal age. However, if you save up money for the purpose of the gospel, those people who are saved by it will welcome you in eternity. What a wise way of doing things!

If we all have such a heart, the Lord's move will be blessed, our number will increase, and the spread will accelerate!

CHAPTER SIX

HOW TO ESTABLISH AND LEAD MEETINGS IN PEOPLE'S HOMES

Scripture Reading: Eph. 5:18-19; Col. 3:16

In this message we will continue to fellowship more thoroughly on the matter of baptism, as this is related to our past exercise and practice. When should a person be baptized? Throughout history Christian groups have had unending debates over this matter. However, if we return to consider the Bible, we will realize that this is actually a simple matter.

THE SCRIPTURAL PRACTICE CONCERNING BAPTISM

As to baptism, the Bible tells us in a simple and clear way, "He who believes and is baptized..." (Mark 16:16). This indicates that believing and being baptized are the two footsteps of one full step. When the Chinese talk about taking a step, they actually mean one foot followed by the other foot. One full step is one footstep followed by the other footstep. Believing and being baptized are the two footsteps of one complete step: believing is one foot, and being baptized is the other, and these make one complete step. Hence, the one step to salvation is to believe and to be baptized. Seldom does a person move one foot, wait five minutes, and then move the other foot. However, we have the erroneous concept that after a person hears the gospel and even prays, he should not be baptized right away since he is probably not clear about the truth and may not quite understand the meaning of salvation. I also had this concept when I was young. According to the Bible, however, every saved person at the time of baptism is not clear about the truth, because he has not had the time to become clear. He believes and right away he is baptized.

Suppose there is a person who hears the gospel, expresses repentance, and also prays and desires to believe. Would you consider such a one as having believed? If you say that his faith is superficial and not thorough enough, then what kind of faith is sufficiently thorough? At the time Paul met the Lord Jesus on his way to Damascus and believed, was he very clear? The Epistle to the Romans was not written to "those who believed yet were not baptized," nor was it written to "those who were not clear regarding salvation and therefore were not yet baptized." Rather, it was written to "all who are in Rome,...the called saints" (1:7). This Epistle says, "Or are you ignorant that all of us who have been baptized into Christ Jesus have been baptized into His death?" (6:3). This indicates that the saints in Rome, who had already been called and sanctified unto God, still did not know that their being baptized was to be baptized into the Lord's death. Not only so, another verse says, "For if we have grown together with Him in the likeness of His death, indeed we will also be in the likeness of His resurrection" (v. 5). This indicates that the saints in Rome also did not know that to be baptized into the Lord's death was to be baptized into the Lord's resurrection. In reality, not only the saints in Rome were not clear about the truth regarding baptism; even many pastors in Christianity today do not know that to be baptized is to be baptized into the Lord's death and into the Lord's resurrection.

What I speak is based upon my experiences. I absolutely believe that on the day I was saved, I was truly saved. As I was walking down the street that afternoon, I looked up to the heavens and said, "O God, I want only You. Even if the whole world were given to me, I do not want it. From now on I want to be a person who preaches Jesus." However, if you were to ask me at that time whether I was clear about salvation, I definitely would have said that I was not clear, and regarding the truth I was even less clear. If you had been there, should you have baptized me? What if I was not saved? You would have baptized a tare, a false Christian, into the church. Would you have acted too fast?

In addition, please consider this: From the day that I was saved, I loved to read the Bible. I was born in Christianity, grew up in Christianity, and also received my education in Christianity, but formerly I never liked to read the Bible. At that time I was zealous for Christianity. If anyone opposed Christianity, I would be the first to fight back. If anyone opposed the Bible, I would also be the first to react. However, as yet I had not believed; I did not read the Bible and definitely did not pray. Nevertheless, on that particular afternoon I got saved. From then on I loved to read the Bible seriously, intensely, and perseveringly. I read whether I understood it or not. Within the two months of my summer vacation, I had read through the Old and the New Testaments once. Then I immediately proceeded to buy spiritual books, trying my best to collect them. As soon as I got my hands on a book, I would read it immediately; I never put it aside until the next day. After reading many books on truths, I then went to the Brethren to be taught. They have the best knowledge of the Bible and the best understanding of the truths. Finally I came into the Lord's recovery and was raised up by the Lord to speak for Him. However, half a year later, I still did not know that there was this word in Romans 6: "Or are you ignorant that all of us who have been baptized into Christ Jesus have been baptized into His death?" (v. 3).

Not only was I this way, but you also were probably the same. After being saved for many years, you finally saw this word in the Bible: "Or are you ignorant that all of us who have been baptized into Christ Jesus have been baptized into His death?" Thus, if we say that a person who is about to be baptized ought to have an understanding of salvation and be clear about the truth, that understanding and comprehension would probably be quite limited. To what extent must he understand and be clear? Take me as an example. From April 1925, when I was saved, until today has been a total of sixty years and four months. During this time I have been reading the Bible diligently every day. If you ask me today, "Brother Lee, are you clear about the truth?", I still cannot say that I am absolutely clear. Hence, if we have the standard that one must be clear concerning the truth and have an understanding of salvation, perhaps for me to be baptized even today is too soon. If we go by this traditional concept, there will be trouble.

When, therefore, can we baptize people? If we study the Bible, we will see that when a person believes is the time he is to be baptized. There is no waiting. In the New Testament, especially in the book of Acts, we cannot find an example of a person who, after he had believed in the Lord, prayed, repented, confessed, and acknowledged the name of the Lord, still could not be baptized but needed to wait awhile. On the contrary, every example clearly shows us that after a person believed, he immediately was baptized.

I was the one leading the church in Taipei at the beginning, and consequently it was I who brought in the "baptism interview." My family formerly belonged to the Baptist Church, a denomination that practices "baptism examinations." However, when people are together for a while, they often develop a dislike of one another; this was so in my case when I saw that the Baptist Church belonged to the Americans. I became disgruntled and went to the Chinese Christian Church, a Presbyterian denomination that belonged to the Chinese. When I went there, I was "examined for baptism." The chief examiner was one of the board directors of a school I had attended in the past and was also the father of one of our former co-workers. One elder asked me, "Mr. Lee, have you believed in the Lord?" I said that I had believed in the Lord. As another elder was about to continue the questioning, a pastor testified, saying, "Mr. Lee's mother is a member of the Baptist Church. His sister also loves the Lord very much. Now he too has risen up to love the Lord." The elder who was the chief examiner continued, "This Mr. Lee is not bad. I do not see any problem; he can be baptized." At that time I said, "Thank God!" for I thought that if they had asked me questions concerning the truth, I probably could not have answered any. I had not read the Bible nor prayed. All the more, I had not repented or confessed. Yet I passed the baptism exam.

Due to that situation in the early days, I felt that it was not proper to baptize people hastily. Things should not be done that way; they must undergo a baptism interview, a thorough talk. This was my intent, but unexpectedly, when the fellowship was put into practice, the brothers and sisters actually began to examine people by asking one by one, "Have you believed? Do you know who Jesus Christ is? Is He God the Father, God the Son, or God the Spirit?" Those who did not pass were ushered into another room where they were told, "Since you do not know the fundamental truths regarding the Trinity, please come back next time. Please be sure you can answer correctly the next time." To be sure, the people came again and answered correctly, and right after they passed the test, they were baptized. Today I am here criticizing myself. That practice was under my leading; it was truly wrong.

Even though there was the practice of the "baptism interview," was everyone who was baptized a real believer? Were there false ones among those baptized? I dare not say; it is for the Lord to judge. Some whom we thought were very good at the time of baptism later turned out to be the worst, while some we thought were not very good at the time of baptism turned out all right. Then there were others who were very good at their baptism but were good only for the next fifteen years. You might have said that a backsliding one was not thoroughly saved. However, after half a year he may come back to the church life, waking up at 5:30 every morning to read the Word and pray, while you as an elder are still not up at 6:30. How can you compare people just by looking at outward practices?

Having had these experiences, I have the boldness at this time to change the system. I am now able to tell you based on the Bible that once a person confesses the Lord's name, prays, and repents, we should baptize him. The Bible says, "Whoever calls upon the name of the Lord shall be saved," and also, "How then shall they call upon Him into whom they have not believed?" (Rom. 10:13-14). The truths in the Bible are so profound that one cannot grasp them in only one or two days. Some criticize that this method is very dangerous. We may preach the gospel for one minute; then a person hears, is moved, prays, and confesses, and immediately we take him to the bathtub to be baptized, immersing him under the water and pouring water upon him. Some say this method is too quick and too risky. However, it is right to baptize people quickly; what is wrong with it? What would be wrong is to neglect him after baptism, not caring whether he lives or dies.

BEGETTING BEING FOLLOWED
BY NURTURING AND TEACHING

A full-term child is born after being in the mother's womb for nine months, but doctors also know that a child born after only six and a half months can also live. Nevertheless, whether a child is born full term or premature, he will die if you neglect him after birth. The mistake we make in our practice today is that we neglect people after we baptize them, just as someone may neglect a child after birth. Begetting but not nurturing is our greatest fault.

After a child is born, he must be nurtured to grow properly. When my youngest daughter had her first boy, both my wife and I were very happy as we went to the hospital to see them. We hoped that the boy would be healthy and chubby. But when we got to the nursery, we found him to be very tiny. My wife and I eyed each other thinking, "How can this child survive? Is there any hope that he will live?" However, today he has grown up very well; he is tall and strong, and he won first place in soccer at school. Though he was born weak, he is healthy and strong today because he was properly cared for and nourished to grow up into such a big boy. In height, weight, and strength, he surpasses many of his age. Hence, nourishment is a very important matter.

A child after birth must not only be nurtured but must also be taught. In this way, he can grow up to be an adult. Therefore, after a person is baptized, the first thing we must do is to enter into an agreement with him, telling him, "From today on we will often visit you at your home, bringing the meeting to you." Then you have to be faithful to feed him, to visit him every week, fifty-two times a year, after his baptism. If you practice this way, do you think that this baptized person will be saved or not? Someone may say, "He was not saved when he was baptized, but he got saved after baptism through our nurturing and teaching until he became clear." It may be that he became clear about salvation only after a certain time, but his need of becoming clear is merely your own criterion. In God's view, there is no such criterion. God's Word says that if the gospel is preached to a sinner, and he receives it, repents, confesses, believes in the Lord Jesus, and also prays, then in the eyes of God he is saved. His spirit has been regenerated.

Actually, the truth regarding salvation is not simple. According to the Bible, salvation is rather involved; it involves a procedure, a process. There is the salvation of the spirit (John 3:5-6), the salvation of the soul (1 Pet. 1:9), and the salvation of the body (Phil. 3:21; Rom. 8:23). If you ask me today, "Have you been saved?", I would have to ask what you mean. My spirit has already been regenerated and saved, my soul is undergoing transformation in the process of salvation, but my body is still the body of an old Chinese man without any change and is not yet saved. In this age, we can receive the salvation of our soul. The salvation and redemption of our body will not be accomplished until the Lord Jesus comes back. At that time our salvation will be complete.

ENTERING INTO AN AGREEMENT
WITH A NEWLY SAVED ONE
TO SET UP A MEETING IN HIS HOME

When a person hears the gospel, repents, confesses, prays, calls on the Lord, and receives the Lord, this is the beginning of his salvation. However, we must not stop there. Rather, we have to continue to feed him and teach him, not allowing him to remain in his original condition. We must immediately care for him and nurture him, just as we would a child after he is born. If we wait a few days to care for a newborn, he will die. In the same way, after a person is baptized, we must immediately make an appointment with him within that week to set up a certain day to visit him and nourish him weekly. This is to enter into an agreement with him.

Following this, we must lead him to open his home for meetings. This is one thing that we must help others to do. As we talk to the new ones, we must lead them to open up their homes for meetings. This is a very important step which we have neglected in the past. Formerly our emphasis had only

been to contact and gain an individual. Now we have seen
that what is more dependable is not the gaining of an individual but the gaining of his household. The sphere of gaining
an individual is too narrow; the gaining of a household is
much broader. Therefore, after much research at this time,
our conclusion is that the unit of gaining people is not the
individual but the household. We also have seen that this is in
accordance with the teaching in the Bible.

In the Old Testament, Noah's salvation was not of one
individual but of his household of eight people. On the day of
the Passover, the Israelites did not have one lamb per person
but one lamb per household. In the New Testament the Lord
said to Zaccheus, "Today salvation has come to this house"
(Luke 19:9). The Philippian jailer asked Paul, "What must I
do to be saved?" Paul said, "Believe on the Lord Jesus, and
you shall be saved, you and your household" (Acts 16:30-31).
Moreover, in the example of Cornelius, the angel told him,
"Send men...and send for Simon, who is surnamed Peter, who
will speak words to you by which you shall be saved, you
and all your house" (11:13-14). These examples indicate that
God takes the believer's household as the complete unit of
salvation.

We did not do an adequate gospel work in the past because
we took the individual as the unit of salvation. Consequently
we suffered loss. From now on we must take the household as
the unit. When we contact people, we contact not only the
individual but also his household. When we knock on doors,
we are knocking not only on the doors of men's hearts but also
on the doors of households. We need to always have this as
our goal. After a person is baptized, our speaking with him
should emphasize the opening of his home for meetings. This
is the gospel secret that we must learn. May the Lord have
mercy on us at this time so that through this secret all of us
may become revived.

Once a home is opened for a meeting, we need to grasp the
opportunity to set up a time for the next meeting. Anyone
who opens the door of his home to us is willing to talk to us
and is desirous for us to visit again. It does not matter
whether he is just trying to be polite; as long as he says,

"Come again when you have time," that is good enough. We should simply grab on to this word and take the opportunity to set up a time with him, saying "Yes, not only are we willing to come again, but we would like to come many more times. Can we decide on a time right now?" In this way, the time is set. With a set time, that home can be considered as opened. Hence, the first visit is to gain a person individually, but after he has been gained, we should immediately set up a time to meet again in his home, to open up his home, so that a further step can be taken to gain his whole household. We must practice this matter until we become skilled.

Recently, a brother from a certain locality testified that only about seventy people went out door-knocking, but within a few days they had visited five hundred homes. The brothers from another nearby locality visited more homes, over one thousand. Even though all the people prayed, the brothers did not have the confidence to baptize them. It is not that those people lacked faith; rather, those who preached the gospel did not have the knowledge or the faith. This is our pitiful condition. We are always hoping that there will be someone to testify for a person, to recommend him; then we will feel confident to baptize him, considering this the safe way. Actually, whether it is safe or not does not depend on others' testimonies but totally on our cooperation with the Lord and on the Lord's grace and mercy. Therefore, as long as a person believes and prays, we should immediately baptize him. If you say, "We might baptize a false one," I would answer, "Many after baptism are eventually found to be real; whereas after a certain delay, the real ones whom you would not baptize, are found to be false ones." Baptism is not a small matter; it is a matter of life and death. How a person turns out depends on this one's baptism. Therefore, we need to know what to do and how to do it properly. What the Chinese consider as the ideal time to cook something is very important. In the same way, you must grab the opportunity to baptize a person. Then after baptism, you must set up a time with him. Once the meeting time is decided, his home is open, and you have the opportunity to gain his household.

LEARNING TO USE THE BIBLE AND
SPIRITUAL PUBLICATIONS TO BRING PEOPLE
TO SALVATION AND TO NOURISH THEM

Next, we need to learn to use the Bible and spiritual publications to nourish people. From the time we begin to contact people, we must learn not to speak idle words, common words, or our own words. The best thing is to read a good book, especially the Bible. The Bible is the world-renowned classic of classics and is the highest book in the human race. Although people may not believe it and may even oppose it, they still would admit that the teachings in the Bible are the highest. When you go to contact someone, you should open the Bible and read a few verses to him. It is especially good to read our Recovery Version because there are footnotes for all of the crucial verses. When you read the important verses to someone and then read the footnotes with him, he will definitely be touched. Once he is stirred up inwardly, you can then explain the footnotes to him, and he will surely be receptive.

Besides the Bible, we still have many spiritual publications such as *The Mystery of Human Life*. This title elicits respect, and the content is not something common. It is not about going to heaven; that is too shallow. *The Mystery of Human Life* is the key to open up people's hearts. This booklet stirs up people's interest, causing them to want to read it, to discover something uncommon and to see the mystery of the four keys. Whether you read it to a person or he reads it himself, you need to observe his facial expression. Once you detect that there is an opening in him, stop reading and ask him directly how he feels. Then ask him to pray with you. Once he prays in the name of the Lord, he is saved. However, there is another half step, the other foot, which is baptism. At this time, you must quickly get the water ready, not giving him any chance to have second thoughts, and baptize him immediately. As soon as he is baptized, it is as if you have made a contract and had it signed. Later, when you meet with him in his home, you must continue the use of the Bible and spiritual publications. When you are meeting in the home meetings with him, you must observe in what areas he is lacking. Once you sense the lack in a certain area, you must immediately find pertinent messages and go over them with him to nourish and to perfect him.

Among us are a large number of spiritual publications, close to one thousand, on all kinds of topics. Every message is appealing. We need to choose appropriate publications and carry two or three with us. We also need to prepare ourselves by finding a few suitable verses; this is to learn how to use the Bible. Then when you go to the next level of visitation, you should not begin with idle words but rather say to him, "This Bible verse is very good. Please read it." According to my experience, eight out of ten people after reading it would say, "I want to buy this book. I want to have this Bible."

LEARNING TO TAKE THE LEAD IN SINGING HYMNS AND PRAYING IN THE HOME MEETINGS

There are two other matters we need to learn: to teach the new believers to sing hymns and to teach them to pray. We all know that however Christian meetings are conducted, four things are involved: the Spirit, God's word, hymns, and prayers. Ephesians 5:18 and 19 say, "And do not be drunk with wine, in which is dissoluteness, but be filled in spirit, speaking to one another in psalms and hymns and spiritual songs, singing and psalming with your heart to the Lord." Verse 18 mentions the spirit, and verse 19 mentions hymns. When we are filled with the spirit from within, we use psalms, hymns, and spiritual songs to speak, sing, and psalm to one another. The emphasis here is not on psalming but on speaking to one another. Speaking to one another indicates that this is in the setting of a meeting. Perhaps you may say that this is a husband and wife speaking to one other at home. Even so, it is still in the setting of a home meeting. As soon as a husband and wife speak to one other, there is a home meeting. What is the content of their speaking to one another? It is the Lord's grace. How do they express it? It is by speaking psalms, hymns, and spiritual songs. In addition, we should also have singing and praying. When these four things are used together, the meeting will definitely be living and wonderful.

THE FOUR CRUCIAL ELEMENTS OF A MEETING—
THE SPIRIT, THE WORD, PRAYER, AND SINGING

We should have the exercise of these four matters not only in the home meetings but also in the big meetings. In our big meetings we do not have adequate exercise of these four matters. We are especially inadequate in the exercise of our spirit. When the church in Los Angeles met at Elden Hall, from 1967 to 1970, whenever the time to meet approached, the saints would begin singing as they walked down the street. In those days the meetings started while the brothers and sisters were still at home. The saints began their meeting before they left home, singing and praying. The meetings officially began at 7:30, but before 7:00 the saints would enter in groups into the meeting hall, singing and shouting with spontaneous praying and reading of the Word. Nowadays, the brothers and sisters probably are not accustomed to this. Some may even disdain it, asking, "Why is there so much noise? Is this worshipping God? Isn't this shouting and yelling like a ball game or a concert?" However, the Bible clearly says that we should shout for joy and praise loudly before the Lord (Psa. 96:12; 98:8; 132:16; Isa. 12:6).

For our spirits to be released, we cannot behave ourselves too properly. Our proper behavior easily kills our spirit. Of course, we should not be wild and crazy; this results in disorder and the loss of self-control (Acts 19:23-40). However, to be quiet is dead; it is not right. To shout and jump in a disorderly way is "crazy"; it is also not right. It is not a matter of being quiet or of shouting and jumping but of the release of the spirit. If the spirit is not released, it is wrong; if the spirit is released, it is right. Once the spirit is released, people are enlivened, and the meeting is also living. If the spirit is not released, people are deadened, and the meeting is also dead. When some people walk into a meeting, they give others the sense that they are icy cold, like blocks of ice from the Arctic Ocean. In such a case, the whole meeting becomes cold. There are others who walk into the meeting and cause the whole meeting to be warmed up. Therefore, the condition of the meeting depends wholly on our individual condition.

As it is in the big meetings, so it is in the home meetings.

It is especially the case when we go to visit others in their homes. Each household has perhaps only three or four people, or at most, five or six. If you are one who is filled with the Spirit and overflowing with the Spirit, as you enter a home, everyone will be able to "smell the holy wine" on you and be affected by your passion. You will sing hymns with enthusiasm, read the Word with enthusiasm, and speak with enthusiasm. Your enthusiasm will touch others, move others, and cause the entire home meeting to be living.

The Spirit, the Word, prayer, and singing are the four crucial elements of a meeting. Not only should we know the Bible, know the spiritual truths in our spiritual publications, and exercise to have a burning spirit, but also we need to learn to sing good hymns. Regarding these four items of the Spirit, the Word, prayer, and singing, I confess that I can boast in the first three items, but I am short in the matter of singing, for I cannot carry a tune. Strangely, however, it does not matter even if you are off key; you should simply exercise to sing loudly. Sometimes your singing is wrong, but those who are musically gifted can correctly learn the song after following you for a while. As he is singing correctly, you are also in tune. Perhaps the elderly saints would say that this is asking too much of them, even to the extent of killing them. We should not be afraid. Doing something that "kills" us may turn out to be life-saving to us. When we do it, it works. Thus, we need to learn to sing hymns earnestly.

SINGING BEING THE BEST WAY TO NOURISH THE NEW ONES

To teach the new ones to sing the hymns is the best way to nourish them. May we all learn to sing hymns. After the time we go to someone's home to baptize him, the next time we meet in his home we can begin to teach him to sing. After singing only four or five times, he will be infused and nourished by the hymns. He may have children at home. When you sing, they may not sing, but after you leave, they will start singing. By singing a little, the truths in the hymns will gradually enter into them.

Singing is also the best "appetizer." If the singing at the

beginning is good, then the home meeting that follows will cause the whole family to be happy. Hence, the home meeting should not begin in a rigid way of social interaction. Do not engage in meaningless small talk, such as how the weather is hot or cold and whether or not to wear warm clothes. Simply sing hymns and learn to teach the family to sing. The hymns among us are especially wonderful. As we sing, our spirits are stirred. Singing is more effective than giving a sermon, and the result is also better.

TEACHING NEW ONES HOW TO PRAY ACCORDING TO THE CONTENT OF THE HYMN

After teaching the new ones to sing, you should continue to help them to pray using the phrases in the hymns. Never have a new one repeat your prayer sentence by sentence; that is a tradition and a formality. You may say a prayer first and then ask him to follow your way. You may pray, "Lord, thank You. In tenderness You sought me, weary and sick with sin" (*Hymns,* #1068). Then have him continue in prayer. In this way you will teach him to pray.

DOING ALL THINGS BY THE SPIRIT AND MOVING BY THE LORD

In leading a home meeting, you need to have variations, to be living and flexible. Do not be set and rigid. What we have fellowshipped here is just one of the many ways. If you are willing to learn to practice, you will become more and more skillful and flexible. You will know that all kinds of changes can be made as long as the spirit is living. If you lead the home meetings in such a way, I believe that the whole family of the new one will receive what is presented. After you leave, they will reminisce and have further fellowship. Therefore, you should never think that we are using gimmicks and wasting our effort. As long as we have the spirit, what we do will not be in vain, and they will receive what we say.

Next, we have to lead the members of the household to learn to pick up the responsibility in the meeting. However, this must not be rigidly enforced. Perhaps the next time you go, you may say, "I am so happy to be here with you all. Sister, can you lead us in singing this time? We can sing the hymn from the last time. Brother, can you lead us to read the Bible? We can read the section that we read last time." Afterward, ask the wife to give a testimony. It may seem as if you are talking to them; actually you are having them share the responsibility of the meeting. The result of leading the home meeting in this way is that they will know how to meet as a home meeting.

The most important thing is that you never allow these things to become a rigid and ritualistic practice. Before you go to a home meeting, you must have ample and living fellowship with the Lord and have thorough confession and prayer until you are filled inwardly. If your spirit is filled with the Lord and His word and you can sing and pray, then you are living, and whatever you do will be living. Whatever a living person does is living; for him, even a dying business will become booming. If a person is dead, however, even a booming business will become dead. We must learn to practice according to this principle.

We need to pay attention to the areas in which we are not living, in which we are too rigid. In these areas we must be alert and diligent to be exercised. We may take the Chinese-speaking meeting in a certain locality as an example. After singing a hymn in the Lord's table meeting, everyone begins to speak the hymn to one another, making the hymn so good and living. However, in the meeting for reading the Word, everyone becomes dumb and quiet, not knowing what to say. Then when it is time to read the spiritual publications, it is done stiffly and without spirit. The hymns are spoken, and the Word and the spiritual publications are also spoken, but why are the two speakings so different? This is due to habit. Once we fall into a habit, our spirit is killed. This is a dreadful matter.

Therefore, I hope that the brothers and sisters will be careful in whatever they do. Do not fall into a habit. You must be living in whatever you read and always exercise the spirit. Never think that since you often read the Bible and the spiritual publications that you know how to read them. Once you rely on your habit, your spirit will be killed. Only with the exercise and the release of the spirit will we be able to read in a living way. As it is in the big meetings, so it should also be in leading the home meetings.

CHAPTER SEVEN

HOW TO BRING PEOPLE INTO
THE CHURCH LIFE

Scripture Reading: 1 Tim. 2:4; 3:15; 2 Tim. 2:2, 15

THE MEANING OF BAPTISM

In the fresh leading we have received of the Lord, our first step is to learn to visit people by door-knocking. This is not door-pounding but door-knocking. Door-pounding implies a rough attitude, whereas door-knocking indicates a polite visit. The first thing with door-knocking is to talk to people about the Lord, to speak the gospel, to lead them to pray and receive the Lord, and then to baptize them. Before a person is baptized, we need to tell him clearly that as we baptize him, we will be immersing him into water, which signifies that we are immersing him into the Lord (Gal. 3:27). Through this, he will experience dying and being buried together with the Lord (Rom. 6:3-5). He was formerly outside of the Lord, but now through baptism he becomes one who is in the Lord. Not only so, we are also baptizing him into the Triune God, that is, into the Father, the Son, and the Holy Spirit (Matt. 28:19) as well as into the church, the Body of Christ (1 Cor. 12:13). This Body is joined to the Lord as one spirit (6:17). Hence, through baptism, we put him into the Lord's death, into the Lord, into the Triune God, and into the church, the Body of Christ. He by faith receives the Lord; we by faith baptize him. This is the simple meaning of baptism.

BELIEVING THAT WE HAVE GAINED SOMEONE
AND THUS GAINING HIM

Many times when we preach the gospel to people, it is not

the listeners but we who do not believe. In our hearts we may say, "This is too fast; it is not going to work." To be sure, then, it does not work. Such is the way in which faith operates. When faith says, "It is done," God says, "Amen; it is done." Our God is amazing. Sometimes He does not say amen right away. He may wait five days before saying, "It is done." However, this does not mean that nothing is happening during those five days. Rather, He works continuously until it is done. This is to bring people to salvation and unto the Lord. Therefore, we all have to learn to only believe and not fear.

THE GOSPEL TAKING THE FAMILY AS THE UNIT

After we help someone to be saved, we must grasp the opportunity to set up a time with this new believer for another meeting. The next time that we visit him is to establish a meeting in his home. This is because the target of our gospel is to gain not the individual alone but rather the whole family as the unit. The multiplication by families is inexhaustible. A Chinese proverb says that cousins span three thousand miles. There are cases of Chinese people immigrating to America, getting their citizenship in five years, and then bringing over their wives, children, parents, siblings, and other relatives. With the son comes his parents and children, with the daughter-in-law, her parents, and with the siblings, their wives. In a few years the whole family has immigrated to America. We must preach the gospel in the same way—not to only one individual but to the entire family. As soon as his home opens up, all of his close and distant relatives will come along. Thus, the multiplication of the gospel is without end.

For this reason, after helping a person to start having meetings in his home, we need to remind him after one or two times, "Brother, you have received the grace of the Lord and are overflowing with joy and blessing. However, God does not want to bless you alone. He also wants to bless your household. He has poured Himself not only on you. He wants to flow into your whole family also. This is marvelous, so you must not hoard this heavenly grace to yourself, not letting it go. You should propagate this grace to your whole family, including all of your distant relatives, by delivering it to their homes." We need to exhort him in this way. However, we should not expect results the following day. Of course, we also should not be in unbelief but should admonish him steadfastly and continually until he is touched. In this way, within just two or three years, his relatives and friends will become linked to us, becoming our gospel targets.

THE TRADITIONAL KILLING WAY AND THE ORGANIC NEW WAY

What should we do in the home meetings? Generally speaking, there are only four things in the Christian meetings: the Spirit, the Word, singing, and praying. The most important of these four is the Spirit. Where the Spirit is, that meeting is living; where the Spirit is not, that meeting is dead. Meeting by meeting we should become more living. The more we exercise our spirit, the more Spirit we will have, and the meetings will become more powerful. In the past, influenced by our naturalness and the poison from traditional Christianity, we always made God's salvation altogether a religious ceremony. As a result, the meetings became dead and tasteless.

By reading church history, we know that the best European architecture from the Middle Ages was the cathedrals. These are steep and pointed on the outside and dark and gloomy on the inside. The use of stained glass windows creates a sense of subdued lighting so that a person on entering feels solemn and reverent, being afraid to sit improperly or even to take a breath. This is Satan's way of killing the believers' function. The record in the four Gospels reveals that in His ministry, the Lord preached to people primarily in the wilderness and secondarily in the homes. One of the first homes used by the Lord was that of Matthew the tax collector. As a tax collector, Matthew was a vile sinner in people's eyes, yet the Lord called him. After he was touched and saved, the first thing he did was immediately to open up his house for a feast, inviting all of his colleagues and friends to come and eat with the Lord Jesus and His disciples. When the Pharisees saw this, they murmured to the Lord's disciples, "Why does your Teacher eat with the tax collectors and sinners?" When the Lord heard this, He turned and gave a word of reprimand to them (Matt. 9:9-13). The Lord also ate in the homes of at least two other Pharisees. One occasion is recorded in Luke 7:36, and the other in Luke 11:37. In addition, the Lord feasted at the home of Martha and Mary, went to the home of Peter's mother-in-law, and visited many other homes to heal the sick and preach the gospel.

When people enter a cathedral, they become solemn and reverent but do not feel secure. However, when they enter a home, instead of fear they sense the warmth of the home. Therefore, we must understand that the traditional way of church services in Christianity is of the devil's teaching with the aim to kill people so that their mouths are shut. The Bible shows us that when the believers come into the meetings, they should have their mouths wide open and must speak. If we were to have a meeting here today, then even before the leading ones arrive and before anything has been written on the board, we ought to have our mouths opened to praise, to sing with rejoicing, or to pray aloud. Surely in this way the meeting will be living.

If a Christian never opens his mouth or functions in the meetings, he will become a dead member. My wife once said that if I do not speak for a month, my legs cramp, my back aches, and I do not sleep well. Therefore, she told me, "You need to hold conferences frequently. As soon as you open your mouth, your legs have no cramps, your back stops aching, you sleep well, and you have a good appetite." This is the normal condition of a Christian. Some elderly ones in their eighties are not able to do anything. They cannot understand much, they are often forgetful, and they are afraid of getting lost when they leave the house. Because of this, they lock themselves at home every day. Today not only do I not get lost, but I can still remember verses from the Bible very well, and my mind is very lucid. This is because not only do I have the Lord in me, but I also exercise my spirit often, release my spirit, and function.

I was born into Christianity, under bondage there for more than twenty years. Once I jumped out of that sphere, I never wanted to be in it again. We oppose the way traditional Christianity meets. (But this does not mean that we can be unrestrained.) Christians are living and joyful; therefore, we do not want dead silence in religion. We hope that the sisters serving to play the piano would come early to every meeting. In this way, when the saints arrive, they can call hymns and begin to sing. Hymns are the easiest way to stir up our spirit because they are the expressions of the poets' sentiments. Take, for example, "Give up the world, Christ to obtain" (*Hymns,* #1025). In the summer of 1948 I was in Shanghai, busy and tired from the work. One day some co-workers and I arranged to go to a park for a rest. It was then that this hymn was written. Whenever we sing this hymn in the meetings, our tiredness easily goes away and our spirits are refreshed. Sometimes you may be the first to come to the meeting. Even though you are only one person, you can start a hymn, playing and singing to yourself. As the brothers and sisters arrive one by one, they can join you in the singing. In this way, the meetings spontaneously will be enlivened.

There is no set agenda in the meeting. After singing, the saints can share from their enjoyment of the hymn and then read a few verses from the Bible, speaking and declaring aloud one to another. It should not always be the same few elders doing the reading, for in doing so, they are going beyond their duties and functioning as "priests" in your place. The brothers and sisters must all exercise to function organically in the meetings, singing and reading the Word in an organic way.

THE CRUCIAL ELEMENTS OF THE MEETING

We have already seen that the Spirit, the Word, singing, and prayer are the four crucial elements of the meetings. The meetings of the Christians are all related to these four matters. When you have these, the meetings spontaneously become living. The first two of the four are nouns, while the latter two are from verbs. We have the Spirit and the Word of the Lord, and in the meetings we must exercise to sing and to pray. I do not sing very well, but I like to sing because it fills me with feeling and enjoyment. When I sing, "In tenderness He sought me, / Weary and sick with sin," the feeling is so sweet. This was exactly my condition sixty-one years ago. I was weary and sick with sin, gambling, watching Chinese opera, and playing soccer to the extent that I could go without meals. At that very time, "In tenderness He sought me, / Weary and sick with sin, / And on His shoulders brought me / Into His flock again." Therefore, every time I sang this song, I was full of sentiment. Sometimes I would even be moved to tears and would pray with a grateful heart, "Lord, I truly praise You. Formerly I was in a dunghill, and I was a vile sinner, but You delivered me out of that situation. You even gave me the ministry of Your word. I am truly unworthy." I praised Him while weeping before Him.

HOW TO TEACH THE TRUTH IN THE HOME MEETINGS

Specifically, the Word is the sixty-six books of the Bible. We realize from experience that for us to have the Word, we must conscientiously study the truth and then use the truth to teach. In every home meeting, we need to present some items of the truth to the new believers for fifteen minutes, thirty minutes, or even longer. How do we do this? We have many booklets, mostly extracts from the *Life-study of Romans,* and we have four volumes of the new *Life Lessons,* which are very suitable for newly baptized ones to read. We can read the first lesson, "Knowing That You Are Saved," with the new one for him to become clear that he is saved and thus be confirmed in his faith. We do not need to finish the entire booklet with him at once—perhaps half would be sufficient—and then tell him, "Brother, when I leave, you can continue reading the other half with your wife and your children. I will leave with you two or three more booklets. When you have time, you can read them also." Then the next time you visit him, you can read another lesson. This is the way to teach the truth.

However, do not have a set way. Perhaps after a few lessons, you can stop and switch to other booklets. We should have read all of the booklets with titles such as "The Law of the Spirit of Life," "The Three Laws in Romans Seven," "Christ Living in Me," "The Triune God and the Tripartite Man," and "How to Receive the Processed Triune God." All of these titles are very attractive. Each time we go to a home meeting, we should bring seven or eight of these, and depending on the situation, pick one out for the new one to read. In this way, he will receive the truth and have the deep impression that, since we have booklet after booklet of uncommon titles, we are not a simple group of Christians. Once he reads them seriously, the truth will get into him.

Moreover, the most important thing we should always have with us is the Recovery Version of the Bible, so that when needed, we can read a section of the Word and the footnotes with him. Once he hears it and reads it, he will be captured, able to know Christ in an accurate way, and understand the grace of God and the salvation of Christ. Spontaneously he will be drawn to receive the truth. Then not only will he welcome you to his home, but he also will desire that you come more often. After a period of time, he will become perfected to the point that you can take him a step further into *Truth Lessons*. The contents of *Truth Lessons* are not as easy as that of the booklets. The lessons are not only well edited and complete but are also rather extraordinary. Hence, when we are about to teach, we need to spend some time in preparation to find an appropriate way to help the new one get into them easily.

HOW TO LEAD THE NEW ONES TO KNOW THE CHURCH

One matter we need to take heed to is that when we first start to meet with a new one in the home meetings, we must not rush to speak about the church. This is because it is a complicated matter, not easy to understand or to get into. The new one has just been saved; we should not trouble him with this matter but first establish him by using the new *Life Lessons*. Wait until he has some knowledge of the truth and a foundation in the Word; then take him on a step further. As we speak, we should exercise wisdom. Do not speak directly about the church, but rather indirectly tell him of the joy we have in our daily church life, giving him an inkling that will motivate him to be drawn to the church life. Even if the new one were to ask you first, "What is the church life?", still do not say too much. Rather, according to his condition, take him on slowly. If you say too much, he may not be able to understand. As the saying goes, "Haste makes waste." This means it is best to do things slowly and not be in a rush. If within a month you cannot speak to a new one about the truth concerning the church, then wait for half a year. If you still cannot do it in half a year, then wait for one or two years. You must wait for the opportune time to unveil the truth to him little by little.

All the elders in the churches desire that the number of saints in their church meetings would increase more and more. Now in every meeting hall there are full-time serving ones. However, some elders complain that although the full-timers daily report good news of baptizing so many, to this day not a single new one can be seen, and the numbers in the meetings are actually diminishing rather than increasing. Even the full-timers have disappeared; their presence is not visible in the meetings, yet they must be financially supported. Regarding this matter, I would say, be patient and at rest. All farmers know that sowing is not a swift matter. The seeds originally piled in the house can be used to make noodles and bread to last two to three months, but once they are sown, they are gone. However, do not worry; the seeds sown in the fall, after passing through a winter and a spring, produce a rich harvest in May. Therefore, do not say that the seeds that you spent money for and have sown are gone. Just be patient for half a year to a year, and you will see the harvest.

Right now, the new way is still in the experimental stage. About ten thousand have been baptized, with at least one-third becoming remaining fruit. However, these will not become remaining fruit in only one day or even in one year. The outcome of the harvest depends upon how much effort we expend. The sowing work itself requires much labor—here a home, there a home, until very many homes in Taipei are gained and baptized. However, to have the harvest, we need to continue to nourish the new ones with the Word as milk and to perfect them with the truth.

Nevertheless, even if a new one does not take the way of the church, do not be concerned. He is at least saved and has received some perfection in the truth. Meanwhile we ourselves surely must live the church life. In our talk, action, and expression there needs to be the outflow of the rich enjoyment of our church life and of the blessings and benefit that we receive from being in the church life. As we talk to the new one about the church, we should motivate him to incline toward this direction. Once there is the inclination, there is the aspiration. However, do not force him. Rather, let him say, "I hope that one day I can go to a meeting with you to live the church life." When he says this, do not be overly excited and say, "Wonderful! I have been waiting for this for two years." This is the most foolish response. You should follow up by asking him, "We have many meetings: the prayer meeting, the Lord's table meeting, the ministry meeting, and the gospel meeting. Which one of these would you like to attend?" Let him choose; do not initiate to choose for him. If you choose for him, then if he goes and finds it tasteless, he will murmur against you.

We should take people on little by little in this way. Whatever is done needs to be in wisdom and according to the spirit. Always seize the opportunity to enlighten the new one. For example, if he chooses the Lord's table meeting, then you should first tell him the meaning of breaking the bread, the significance of the bread and the cup, and the meaning of the Lord's table. In this way, he will receive the appropriate help so that when he comes to the table meeting, he can enter into it right away. He will taste the Lord's death and resurrection and will enjoy the riches of the Lord. He will be fully satisfied, and not only will he long to come again, but he will also go back to promote it to his family members and bring them with him.

CONTINUING STEADFASTLY IN
PRACTICING THE NEW WAY

This is our way of taking people on. If we cannot accomplish this in one year, we will do it in two years. Do not be in a rush. Rather, continue steadfastly in three things: visit by door-knocking, have home meetings, and teach the truth. Do not set a time limit and say that you will take care of a new one for only three months; then if he does not come along in three months, you will abandon him. In our nourishing and teaching of the new ones, there is no need to keep track of time. Regardless of how long it takes, we will continue to lead a new one into the truth. To do this even until the Lord comes back is worthwhile. Some people are peculiar and bent strangely. If you tell such a one to go east, he will insist on going west; if you ask him to go fast, he will be deliberately slow. It seems that he may not change even when the Lord comes back. Nevertheless, you must still wait patiently and continue to maintain your fellowship with him. This is true not only with new ones but also with the believers who do not come into the church life. If we are willing to be faithful in this way, the Lord will surely reward us when He comes back. He will say to us, "Formerly this child of Mine was not being edified in the truth, but because of your faithfulness, he has been edified."

When we practice this way, we also break three matters. First, we break the concept of most Christians that people in the Lord's recovery are reserved and self-confined. In the past, many have said that we are stealing their sheep. Rather, we are going out to gain new ones, nourish them, care for them, and build them up. In this case, those who criticize us will be silenced and unable to say anything more. Second, we break the "restrictive nature" of the Lord's recovery and manifest the inclusiveness of the church. Whether or not the new ones come to the meetings is their business. We still include them and week by week continue to visit them and have fellowship with them, teaching them the truth. Although they do not come, if we are faithful to teach, one day their children will come. In the past we have had this kind of testimony of children saying to their parents, "Dad and Mom, we are sorry, but we are going to meet with those brothers and sisters who teach us the truth." Third, we break the limitation of our gospel preaching by taking the family of the new ones as the unit and becoming linked to all of their relatives. Forty years ago when I was serving in Chefoo, the service of the church grew to such an extent that even the unbelievers would say that to believe in Jesus they must come to our place.

In the Full-time Training in Taipei, presently there are

over seven hundred saints from various countries. Every day they go out to knock on doors in the morning, afternoon, and evening, baptizing at least one person per week. If these seven hundred gain seven hundred homes per week, there will be twenty-eight hundred homes in one month and eleven thousand two hundred homes in four months. With these families as the units and as the connections to all their relatives, there is no knowing how great the increase can be. Not only will the gospel be widespread, but the truth will be able to be preached and propagated continuously. May we all have such a long-term vision to understand the importance of this kind of practice. Hence, we need to aggressively use *Truth Lessons* and spend the time either to bring people into the church life or to continuously nourish and build them up in their homes. We believe that this labor will not be wasted but will be of great value before the Lord.

HOW TO TEACH THE TRUTH LESSONS

The new way is nothing other than to continue steadfastly in these three matters: to visit people by door-knocking, to raise up or establish meetings in the homes of new ones, and to teach the truth. If the new one is willing to come to the church, we will give him more care, but if he is not willing, as long as he does not refuse us, we will still take care of him in a timely manner. The teaching of the truth should be done sequentially and gradually. It cannot be accomplished once for all. It is better to start by having a new one read the booklets, which are easier to digest. After a period of time when his appetite has been aroused, we can bring him into *Truth Lessons*.

To teach *Truth Lessons* is not an easy matter. When some saints hear "Truth Lessons," their immediate understanding is "to teach." Actually, there is no need for you to teach, because each lesson is a message, and each message is also very rich. What we ought to do is help the new ones read the lessons. This is not to say that there is no need to come to the meetings, that one can simply buy the book and read it at home. In doing this, the proper appreciation or taste will not be developed. In addition, you should not come together and merely have each one read a paragraph—one person reading one paragraph and another person reading another paragraph. That is to read in a dead way, and the more you read, the more you become dead. Hence, the way to read is not simple.

When reading *Truth Lessons,* the most important thing is to read the outlines. You should read not merely by taking turns but in a living way, using your spirit. Sometimes when you come to an important point and you have some experience, you can give a short testimony in three to five sentences. When you have an appropriate hymn, you can choose to sing a stanza. The most needful thing is to exercise your spirit. Initially it may be difficult and not very successful. However, if you continue to practice, you will improve.

It is best to have thirty to fifty people in one class that covers *Truth Lessons.* Not every church has to practice this in the same way. If only a few churches are willing to try, a good practice will evolve, and other churches will learn. Then after a few weeks, all will be able to do it. Human beings are very clever; whatever they see, they learn. Some may not participate but only look on. If they receive a supply in the meetings, eventually they will take the initiative to participate. In the process of teaching, there is no one taking the lead to teach. Rather, the saints should read together in a living way, using their spirit. This gives the Spirit the real opportunity to teach us. The experienced saints must be alert to take the lead to emphasize the main points in the reading. The saints who are touched can give a testimony or point out a hymn. At the end you may be inspired to give a concluding testimony. There is no set way—only do not drag out the singing or the testimonies, because people will not be able to bear it. Some saints love to speak endlessly. When this situation arises, a brother or a sister should immediately stop them. It is better that it not be the leading brother who stops them, because the one speaking may be offended. This is an organic Bible reading—completely organic—without anyone being dictatorial or in control. As to home meetings, three to five people can make up one group, being similarly organic, living and flexible.

A TESTIMONY

A sister, who is a teacher, thought that the principal of the school, who is also a brother, was an amiable person, so she gave him a copy of the Recovery Version and a copy of *Truth Lessons.* He brought them home, but by coincidence, just before he read them, his parents came to visit him. His father, who was in his sixties and already retired, was then meeting with the Baptist Church and had been invited to teach a Sunday school class. He felt hard-pressed, not knowing what to teach, so he collected materials everywhere. That day when he came to his son's house and saw the English version of *Truth Lessons,* he took it and read it. As soon as he read it, he treasured it very much and decided to teach from this book in the Sunday school class. When the principal saw that his father valued and appreciated this book very much, he told the sister who gave him the book. This sister then gave him two more books for him and his wife. One morning at school, the principal asked the sister to come and in tears told her, "I have believed in Jesus for thirty years, but I never knew how the Bible came about. It is by reading *Truth Lessons* that I now know." This shows us that *Truth Lessons* is truly a powerful book for teaching the truth.

THE LORD'S RECOVERY BEING
THE RECOVERY OF THE TRUTH

May the brothers and sisters understand that the Lord's recovery is the recovery of the truth. The Lord's recovery has been among us for sixty-four years. We are not novices. The practice of the new way and the leading in this move today did not come from our imagination but through our experience, our seeking, and our research into history. Therefore, we must receive this new leading. Many elderly saints in Taiwan are accustomed to a big meeting on the Lord's Day morning with the hope of hearing a good message. When the system changed, we did sympathize with them, letting everyone either register freely for the class on *Truth Lessons* or otherwise join the big meeting. At first, the big meeting had almost one hundred people, but as the weeks went by, the number of people became fewer and fewer. It was not that they had quit coming, but they had received a taste of the *Truth Lessons* class, and by that one taste they were caught. Hence, the number in the big meeting decreased, and the number in the *Truth Lessons* class increased. This proves that *Truth Lessons* is able to release the truth and build up the brothers and sisters.

I was the first one to speak in Hall One of the church in Taipei. From 1949 until today has been thirty-seven years. The year before last when I went back to Taipei, I said that some of you have been listening to my speaking for thirty-seven years. Back then you were still young brothers and sisters, and most of you were not yet married. Today even your sons and daughters have graduated from universities and many of them have become elders. Before they were born, you were already listening to my preaching here, but until today you have not graduated from "elementary school." Why do I say this? The human educational research has worked out a system of six years of elementary school, six years of high school, and four years of college, with a set curriculum every year. A person proceeding through this curriculum in a sequential way will definitely graduate from college after sixteen years and will have systematically assimilated the general knowledge prevalent in the human race. However, we have been speaking to you under this roof for these thirty-seven years, mostly according to inspiration and not in a systematic way. Therefore, although you have been listening to this day, you still cannot utter one sentence if I were to ask you to speak on justification by faith. This may be compared to listening to mathematics for thirty-seven years and, even though you know that three plus two is five, when you are asked to go teach others, you do not know how.

We all have to admit that the Lord has given us truths in abundance, and all these truths are pearls and gems. However, we have placed them as "decorations" in our homes, not knowing how to make use of them. If others were to pick up one precious stone, they would treasure it to the uttermost. We, however, have precious stones in abundance like the sand, yet we do not use them nor do we know how to use them. God has said that He "desires all men to be saved and to come to the full knowledge of the truth" (1 Tim. 2:4). Not only have we not carried this out accordingly, but we ourselves do not have the full knowledge of the truth. Paul also said to Timothy, "Be diligent to present yourself approved to God, an unashamed workman, cutting straight the word of the truth" (2 Tim. 2:15). To cut straight implies to unfold the various parts of the Word of God rightly and straightly without any distortion, just as a carpenter cuts wood straightly. We have not practiced this in our midst. This is our great debt to the saints.

ACCEPTING THE CHANGE OF SYSTEM COMPLETELY AND ENDEAVORING TO PRACTICE THE GOD-ORDAINED NEW WAY

Therefore, we are doing our utmost to change the system. There are three parts to the change. The first change is in "begetting," in giving birth to new believers—from the traditional way of waiting for people to come to hear the gospel to the way of visiting people's homes by knocking on their doors to get them saved. The second change is in "nourishing"—from previously going to others' homes simply to talk lightly to using our spirit to speak the word, sing, and pray in order to nourish and cherish the new ones. The third change is in "teaching"—from the old way of preaching in big meetings according to inspiration to the use of proper instructional materials and teaching in a sequential way. We hope that the brothers and sisters understand these three points and accept them completely. Not only must the co-workers and elders do this, but also all the saints must do it.

Due to the new leading that the Lord has given us, we must have an increased number of saints to shoulder the burden to meet the need. The brothers and sisters must all participate and be willing. However, almost everyone is encumbered, some by their businesses and others by the need to work and also to take care of household matters. Their time is consumed, and not much of it can be freed up. Nevertheless, as long as you have the heart, no matter how busy you are, I believe that you can take two to three hours a week to go door-knocking, to nourish the new ones, and to teach them. This is also acceptable. Once on a mountain I met a member of the Jehovah's Witnesses who is in the real estate business. Normally he is extremely busy, but he made the decision to spend two days a week to go door-knocking. We do not expect that every saint will be like him, but we hope that those who have the heart will go to visit not only the familiar ones but also those whom they have never contacted before.

A brother from Cleveland said that in only a few days they knocked on more than one thousand doors. As door-knocking requires a great deal of manpower, many full-timers need to be raised up. I believe that this is the leading of the Lord and absolutely the best practice after years of consideration. For every local church, there should be one full-timer for every twenty saints. There are over five hundred full-timers now in Taiwan, and the number of applicants exceeds eleven hundred. According to the number meeting in the United States, there also should be five hundred full-timers. Presently there are already two hundred, so there is still a shortage of three hundred. Thus, the need is very great.

THE NEED FOR FULL-TIMERS
AND THE FULL-TIME TRAINING

In February of this year, we pointed out that some people are job-dropping full-timers and some are job-keeping full-timers. Every one of us should live entirely for the Lord's interests on this earth. Although you have a job, you are still working for the Lord. This way depends on your taking what you have received from your job, aside from amply supplying the needs of your family, and offering it entirely to the Lord to meet the needs of the work and of the full-timers. This is extremely important and has a bearing on the speed of the advance and spread of the Lord's recovery.

The Full-time Training in Taiwan started on August 12. In order to be accepted, there are three requirements. First, you must have a college degree; second, you must be single without the encumbrance of a family; and third, you cannot be over forty years old. Thus far, there are five hundred applicants from Taiwan, over twenty from the Philippines, one hundred forty-eight from the United States and Canada, thirty-two from Europe, and four from Ghana, Africa. There are also two language teachers from New Zealand. Today the world has become small, so language has become very important. Hence, in the Full-time Training there are five foreign language classes, and there is also a training class for the Chinese language. There are one hundred sixteen teachers taking turns to teach. Generally, one group teaches for a month, and then another group of teachers takes over. In addition, there are twenty to thirty serving ones for special items, such as caring for the medical needs and for the meals in the training center. Thus, there are about seven hundred students and numerous teachers and serving ones residing in Taipei. Hence, this is a great move in the Lord's recovery. Thank the Lord, once the news of the training went out, churches everywhere contributed much to this work. It is estimated that this training will cost about one million U. S. dollars. The churches in Taiwan will pick up the burden for four to five hundred thousand dollars. This shows us that the weight of the burden requires that all the churches over the entire globe be in one accord to ease the load in a coordinated effort.

Regarding the gospelization of Taiwan, we have a set of plans. Starting from January of 1988, one thousand full-timers will be raised up in Taiwan and grouped into one hundred teams of ten to spread into the villages. Each team will go to a village to knock on doors for one month. At least ten to twenty people will be gained in each village. Then after one month a small new church will be produced. Then two from each team will stay to take care of the meetings, while the other eight hundred will form another eighty teams to continue on to eighty other villages, doing the same thing for a month. By doing this for four months, there will be churches established in all of the villages in Taiwan, accomplishing the goal to gospelize Taiwan.

Initially, we said that we would gospelize Taiwan in five years. Many people said, "How is this possible? Where will the twenty-five hundred full-timers come from?" Thank the Lord for His provision! Through the quality educational system, transportation, and economical establishment of the

Taiwan government, Taiwan is now able to produce five hundred full-time brothers and sisters and provide for their support without any lack. Perhaps there is no need to wait until January 1988, but by January or July of next year, 1987, the move to spread the gospel can already begin because many of the full-timers will have had a year of training and will be ready to go. I have also told them that after Taiwan has been gospelized, they will go on to foreign countries, unless the Lord has a special leading. I deeply believe that this tremendous strength will have a great impact in the spread of the Lord's recovery. This is our long-range view. May the Lord fulfill it!

ADVANCING IN CARRYING OUT
THE NEW WAY SEQUENTIALLY, NOT BEING IN A RUSH

We have already seen how, after door-knocking and the establishment of the home meetings, we should lead the new ones into *Truth Lessons* and into the church life. First, we must set up goals, and in carrying them out we must not be in a rush. Rather, we should slowly and sequentially move forward step by step in a steady way. We may use driving as an example. First you may decide that you are going to Los Angeles. There are many ways to get to Los Angeles, and they are different depending on the circumstances. According to the weather and the time, you will pick the safest and the least troublesome way. Similarly, there are many ways to carry out the teaching of *Truth Lessons*. You can teach it home by home, or you can combine three homes and read together. You can have twenty to thirty people or forty to fifty people come together. This all depends on the practical situation. While working it out, understand what is important, pace yourself, move on systematically, and do not be rushed. In this way, you will not suffer loss. Hold on to this principle, adapting and making changes according to the situation. You must always know clearly within yourself how to do it and where to start.

We can also learn from one another through much fellowship. However, not every place can carry things out in the same way. Presently, the Lord's table meeting in the church in

Anaheim is not held in the meeting hall. This may be right and feasible, but not every local church can do this. As far as Anaheim is concerned, this practice did not take place due to a moment's inspiration, nor was it carried out on a day's notice. This came about after more than half a year of exercise, consideration, and research, arriving at the conclusion to have this practice. We should, in all the churches everywhere, consider and learn what to do according to the situation of each church.

LEARNING TO HAVE FELLOWSHIP IN FINANCIAL MATTERS

We have also pointed out that our desire is to have one full-timer for every twenty saints who are meeting and to have the place that produces the full-timers provide for their support. However, the situations in the churches differ. Some local churches are strong financially but are unable to produce full-timers, whereas other local churches have plenty of students, with few earning money, and are unable to support many full-timers. Hence, in the matter of finance, may all the churches around the globe be in one fellowship. We do not have a central financial administration, nor do we wish to have central control. The Bible gives us the best example; that is, there should be much fellowship in financial matters among churches and between meeting halls. Those churches that are rich financially should care for the churches that are lacking. The move of the Full-time Training now and of the expansion in the future not only involves Taiwan and the United States but also India, Burma, and the Arab countries. They are all in this move and should enter into this fellowship.

Looking at the needs in the world, we can do nothing but give our all and be faithful to bring forth one full-timer per twenty persons in order to open up the situation so that our expansion may go forth to meet the need of the Lord's present move. May we be sufficiently strong in what we do, not cutting any corners or hindering God in any way. If we offer up all of our energy and financial capacity, and everyone all over the earth moves in one accord, how much the Lord can bless us! However, we do not have a central administration.

Rather, we have mutual fellowship among the localities. May we all learn to have a good practice in this matter. In the Body there is no pressure or coercion. There are only supply and fellowship.

A CONCLUDING WORD

I hope that the brothers and sisters will receive the points fellowshipped in these messages. The carrying out of the new way ordained by God does not depend solely on the elders and the co-workers. Rather, the whole Body needs to take action— to go door-knocking, to establish meetings in the new ones' homes, and to continue steadfastly in feeding, building up, and teaching the truths. Furthermore, there should be the continuous spread of gaining new homes, one after another. On the other hand, we should also offer up our finances—not only a part but the whole—in order to produce more full-timers for the move to spread the Lord's recovery on this earth.

ABOUT THE AUTHOR

Witness Lee was born in 1905 in northern China and raised in a Christian family. At age 19 he was fully captured for Christ and immediately consecrated himself to preach the gospel for the rest of his life. Early in his service, he met Watchman Nee, a renowned preacher, teacher, and writer. Witness Lee labored together with Watchman Nee under his direction. In 1934 Watchman Nee entrusted Witness Lee with the responsibility for his publication operation, called the Shanghai Gospel Bookroom.

Prior to the Communist takeover in 1949, Witness Lee was sent by Watchman Nee and his other co-workers to Taiwan to ensure that the things delivered to them by the Lord would not be lost. Watchman Nee instructed Witness Lee to continue the former's publishing operation abroad as the Taiwan Gospel Bookroom, which has been publicly recognized as the publisher of Watchman Nee's works outside China. Witness Lee's work in Taiwan manifested the Lord's abundant blessing. From a mere 350 believers, newly fled from the mainland, the churches in Taiwan grew to 20,000 in five years.

In 1962 Witness Lee felt led of the Lord to come to the United States, settling in California. During his 35 years of service in the U.S., he ministered in weekly meetings and weekend conferences, delivering several thousand spoken messages. Much of his speaking has since been published as over 400 titles. Many of these have been translated into over fourteen languages. He gave his last public conference in February 1997 at the age of 91.

He leaves behind a prolific presentation of the truth in the Bible. His major work, *Life-study of the Bible,* comprises over 25,000 pages of commentary on every book of the Bible from the perspective of the believers' enjoyment and experience of God's divine life in Christ through the Holy Spirit. Witness Lee was the chief editor of a new translation of the New Testament into Chinese called the Recovery Version and directed the translation of the same into English. The Recovery Version also appears in a number of other languages. He provided an extensive body of footnotes, outlines, and spiritual cross references. A radio broadcast of his messages can be heard on Christian radio stations in the United States. In 1965 Witness Lee founded Living Stream Ministry, a non-profit corporation, located in Anaheim, California, which officially presents his and Watchman Nee's ministry.

Witness Lee's ministry emphasizes the experience of Christ as life and the practical oneness of the believers as the Body of Christ. Stressing the importance of attending to both these matters, he led the churches under his care to grow in Christian life and function. He was unbending in his conviction that God's goal is not narrow sectarianism but the Body of Christ. In time, believers began to meet simply as the church in their localities in response to this conviction. In recent years a number of new churches have been raised up in Russia and in many eastern European countries.

OTHER BOOKS PUBLISHED BY
Living Stream Ministry

Titles by Witness Lee:

Titles by Watchman Nee:

Available at
Christian bookstores, or contact Living Stream Ministry
2431 W. La Palma Ave. • Anaheim, CA 92801
1-800-549-5164 • www.livingstream.com